Praise for
Love Remembers

"*Love Remembers* is a beautiful read. It highlights important issues encountered on an incredibly difficult journey and how even the most brilliant individuals can be impacted by Alzheimer's. It's a story so many people will relate to."

—**Shelly Young, MS,** program manager for the Alzheimer's
Association, North Central Texas Chapter

"With unwavering honesty, Kathe tells the story of countless moments when faith, love, family, and community transformed chaos into order, darkness into light, and fear into peace. *Love Remembers* is an invaluable source of emotional support and spiritual comfort for those caring for their loved one through the devastating experience of Alzheimer's."

—**Patrick O'Malley, PhD,** grief therapist and author of *Getting Grief
Right: Finding Your Story of Love in the Sorrow of Loss*

"Kathe's story is both candid and heart-warming. It helps the reader process a heart-wrenching diagnosis of Alzheimer's, using faith and hope as a constant guide. As I became immersed in her family's journey, I found myself, at times, reliving our own family's experience with dementia."

—**Gail Snider,** executive director of Dementia Friendly Fort Worth

"From the prologue to the final chapter, *Love Remembers* brings the reader face-to-face with the realities of loving someone with memory loss. Readers will be able to identify with the stages one goes through when grieving the losses faced along the dementia journey. Kathe is transparent in her telling of the struggle that is Alzheimer's and generous with sharing the wisdom and insight she and her family gained."

—**Megan (Mrs. Victor) Boschini,** wife of the chancellor of Texas Christian University

"When I closed the cover of this revealing tribute to family and faith, I felt I'd found a friend. Filled with personal stories of everyday challenges and beautifully written, Kathe's book details her journey of faith and unshakable devotion to a man she vowed to love in sickness and in health. Although he is now in the final stages of this terrifying disease, she is still a student of the magical power of hope. This is Kathe's first book, but I hope it won't be her last."

—**Mary Rogers,** *Book Talk* columnist and freelance journalist

May love bless you beyond words!
♥ Kathe A Goodwin

Love
Remembers

Holding on to Hope and Faith
in the Face of Early-Onset Alzheimer's

Kathe Ambrose Goodwin

RIVER GROVE
BOOKS

This book is a memoir reflecting the author's present recollections of experiences over time. Its story and its words are the author's alone. Some details and characteristics may be changed, some events may be compressed, and some dialogue may be recreated.
The names and identifying characteristics of some persons referenced in this book have been changed to protect their privacy.

This book is intended as a reference volume only. It is sold with the understanding that the publisher and author are not engaged in rendering any professional services. The information given here is designed to help you make informed decisions. If you suspect that you have a problem that might require professional treatment or advice, you should seek competent help.

Published by River Grove Books
Austin, TX
www.rivergrovebooks.com

Distributed by River Grove Books

Design and composition by Greenleaf Book Group and Lindsay Starr
Cover design by Greenleaf Book Group and Lindsay Starr
Cover images used under license from ©istock.com/SasinParaksa; ©pngwing.com

Publisher's Cataloging-in-Publication data is available.

Print ISBN: 978-1-63299-554-4

eBook ISBN: 978-1-63299-555-1

First Edition

For Steve,
for the 6.2 million people in the United States and
the 50 million worldwide
who are living with Alzheimer's disease or
another form of dementia,
and for all those who love them

So faith, hope, love abide, these three;
but the greatest of these is love.

1 CORINTHIANS 13:13 RSV

More than that, we rejoice in our sufferings, knowing that suffering produces endurance, and endurance produces character, and character produces hope, and hope does not disappoint us, because God's love has been poured into our hearts through the Holy Spirit which has been given to us.

ROMANS 5:3–5 RSV

Contents

Prologue

Imagine one day sitting comfortably at home in your favorite chair. You are surrounded by a multitude of familiar belongings, ranging from the functional to the meaningful to those that simply bring you joy. All are a part of who you are. It is easy to take them for granted.

Without warning, an intruder sneaks in. Like a thief in the night, he slowly and methodically begins stealing from you.

At first, you don't even notice. The thief takes things you haven't used in a long time, little items stuffed in the back of junk drawers and overfilled cabinets.

But he isn't satisfied with just that, and he doesn't leave. He gets bolder. He snatches your checkbook and credit cards. Your car keys go missing. He wanders into your closet and rearranges all your clothes—just because he can. He delights in disorder and confusion. And even though you now are aware of his presence, you are powerless to stop him.

Mockingly, he scrambles all the buttons on your television remote and shreds your collection of beloved books. Your favorite pastimes are now gone. When you're hungry and want to use the toaster or microwave, there's no way—all the kitchen appliances along with their instruction manuals are gone too. Long to communicate with the outside world? Impossible. Your computer, phone, and even pens are missing. As if that weren't enough, the thief greedily grabs your watch, clocks, and calendars as well so that time no longer has any meaning. Still, he is not finished.

Ruthlessly, he seizes all your mementos, that precious collection of items you have curated and tightly held on to over a lifetime. And finally, he steals your treasured family photographs, not even sparing the ones with you in the center. Within this earthly realm, he robs you of *you*.

That is what having Alzheimer's disease is like. It is a constant thief. It is the worst kind of thief. It stealthily enters your brain and never leaves . . . until there is nothing left to take. And you and your loved ones are powerless to stop it.

I watched unknowingly as Alzheimer's diabolically altered my father-in-law's behavior, stressing my mother-in-law into a premature death.

I watched sorrowfully as Parkinson's dementia rapidly took what was left from my father at the end of his life.

I watched helplessly as vascular dementia cruelly snatched from my mother her genteel dignity, her coveted wisdom and advice, and her memory that I was her daughter.

And I lived it every moment of every day as early-onset Alzheimer's relentlessly stole piece after piece from my beloved husband.

It brutally stripped us of our planned future with each other and our two children. It painfully left us exposed in ways we never could have envisioned. And it mercifully deepened our family's faith as we increasingly depended on the Lord for guidance, for comfort, and for strength.

The thief comes only to steal and kill and destroy; I came
that they may have life, and have it abundantly.

JOHN 10:10 RSV

CHAPTER 1

Perspective

*Trust in the Lord with all your heart
and lean not on your own understanding . . .*

PROVERBS 3:5 NIV

"Everything looks normal," the neurologist assured us as she pointed to the MRI glaring from the wall. It was an image of my husband's sixty-one-year-old brain.

All at once, I was both relieved and perplexed, as I knew that something inside Steve had changed.

The doctor asked him to walk down the hallway of her office. As he walked, she observed his erect, six-feet-tall stature, long stride, and quick, steady gait that my short legs could never match.

"Looks good. No physical impairments," she said, checking that off her list.

Moving on to the cognitive side of the examination, she handed Steve a piece of blank paper and a pen.

"Draw a clock with the time at two thirty," she instructed. He did nothing.

"I want you to draw me a clock with the hands pointing to two thirty," she repeated. Still nothing.

After hearing the instructions multiple times, he finally drew an irregular circle. That was all. No numbers or clock hands. A blank, misshapen face. The neurologist was clearly taken aback, yet she forged ahead.

In the next mental exercise, she asked Steve to "count backward from one hundred by sevens."

"By sevens," he repeated.

She reiterated, "Backward from one hundred."

"One hundred," he said.

This went on for a couple of minutes, with Steve merely echoing the last number he had heard. Clearly, he was not going to come up with "ninety-three."

Visibly frustrated, the doctor looked at me with a furrowed brow and inquired, "Do you understand what I am asking him to do?"

I nodded slowly, lost in the severity of those moments. Not only had Steve failed to perform as requested, but it was obvious he had not even processed the instructions. The results of the third and final cognitive test, in which the doctor asked Steve to recall three words given to him only a few minutes prior, were equally devastating.

This strong and loving husband and father, this high-powered attorney, this man with a lifelong appreciation of history, literature, and the arts, had just bombed the most basic of mental tests. His mind had failed to perform in executive functioning, attention, and working memory. It was a silent explosion of sorts.

Shaking her head in amazement, the doctor returned her gaze to the MRI and proclaimed, "Now I do believe I see a little shrinkage here on one side of the brain!"

The image was exactly the same. Only, based on this new evidence, her perspective had changed. And with it, my perspective of our family's little corner of the planet was flipped on its axis.

We never saw that neurologist again.

CHAPTER 2

Before the After

Love bears all things, believes all things,
hopes all things, endures all things.

1 CORINTHIANS 13:7 RSV

It's hard not to fall for a guy when he simply asks you to "just stand there and look beautiful." At least that's how it was for me. Steve was my first and only love.

He liked to joke that we met while I was "moving things into his apartment"—hoping to raise an inquisitive eyebrow or two. Those "things" actually belonged to my brother, Jody, who needed a place to live for a few months leading up to his wedding. I helped him move in with Steve. Friends since high school, they had reconnected during law school at Southern Methodist University in Dallas. As a new lawyer, Steve was working at a small local firm, earning a wealth of experience for not much pay. A roommate to share expenses on his two-bedroom apartment was just what he was looking for. A steady girlfriend? Not so much.

It was the summer of 1976, and I had just graduated from Texas Christian University in my hometown of Fort Worth. Several girlfriends and I made the Big Leap thirty miles east to "Big D" to begin careers or, as in my case, post-graduate studies. While I pursued a master's degree in mass communications, Steve began pursuing me.

From that first meeting in his apartment, we had an easy, flirtatious rapport. We began looking forward to seeing each other at the pre-wedding showers and parties for Jody and his fiancée, Patti, who had been my sorority big sister. Even when Steve surprisingly showed up at one party with another girl, we were still unmistakably drawn to each other. Lucky for me they were "just good friends."

Our first official date was in December, one month after Jody and Patti's wedding. He took me to his office Christmas party.

After that, Steve became my guy. I couldn't get enough of this tall, handsome young man—especially when he wore my favorite sweater that made his eyes shimmer green. He had a natural intelligence and curiosity that exceeded even his impressive education. Our conversations were simultaneously effortless and stimulating, covering everything from history and politics to sports and movies. Although he was a bit rhythmically challenged, he lost himself in all kinds of music, from Beethoven to The Beatles to Billy Joel—readily adding my favorite, Barbra Streisand, to the playlist.

Family was at the top of his priorities, as it was for me. The day he entreated me to "just stand there and look beautiful," I was waiting in his apartment to drive him to the airport. Steve was catching a flight to Houston to visit his parents, who had recently moved there. He often made the trip to see them.

Together, he and I enjoyed everything from sitting in church on Sunday mornings with my parents to sitting in a smoke-filled country-western bar on Saturday nights with friends. As impressive as Serious Steve was, Fun Steve was magnetic. Each week, my girlfriends and I looked forward to him guiding us along what we aptly named the "Margarita Trail" in search of the best margarita in town. We never came to a definitive conclusion but enjoyed lots of limes and laughter in the pursuit.

By the time Steve and I got engaged in June 1978, we were both living in Fort Worth. He was an associate at a well-established law firm downtown, and I was writing copy and supervising accounts at a respected advertising and public relations agency. Since we had offices in the same building, my spirits soared whenever we happened to bump into each other in the elevator.

Our beautiful wedding six months later was exactly the way my dear mother planned it. In the old, traditional manner, there was a receiving line at the reception, just as there had been at Jody and Patti's two years earlier. The difference was that in their line, Steve had stood next to me at the end, telling more than a few befuddled guests that he was our "long-lost brother." (I guess he knew even then that he wanted to be a part of our family one way or another!) This time, unmistakably, he was beside me as my husband. I remember my sweet grandmother leaning in to whisper in my ear, "I loved Steve even before you did!"

We soon purchased our first house—a fixer-upper—just around the corner from my parents. While my mother took on the building contractor duties, Steve's mom used her sewing skills to make bedroom curtains out of sheets. Steve and I scraped wall-paper off the dining room walls in the evenings after work and dug up the neglected flower beds on weekends. With our fathers pitching in as well, it truly became the home that family built.

Over the next ten years, Steve's professional career flourished. He made partner by age thirty, developing a stellar reputation from the outset in business litigation and later in corporate reorganization law. Naturally, it wasn't long before he was being recruited by other distinguished firms, both near and far. A mid-sized group in Dallas that Steve admiringly described as "the lawyers' law firm" eventually won him over in the summer of 1988. Thus began his daily forty-five-minute-each-way commute that became our new lifestyle.

Time away from work was spent with family and friends, traveling, cheering on the TCU football team, attending the symphony, exploring museums, volunteering, and never missing a television episode of *Dallas* or *Dynasty*. Multitasking came easily to Steve. He is the only person I have ever known who could watch TV, read a novel, win at solitaire, and carry on a conversation—all at the same time.

After a decade of patiently planning and impatiently waiting for children, we were at last blessed with the extraordinary gift of adoption. Our beautiful baby daughter, Angela, came into our lives, and almost two years later our precious son, Stephen Jr., arrived.

Instantly, Steve became a devoted and doting dad. When the children were little, he delighted in reading to them on the sofa by day and tickling them in bed at night. He was equally at home building a teddy bear with Angela at the mall as he was in a cannonball splash contest with Stephen at the pool. In church, he wrapped his arms around them as we sang our favorite closing hymn, "Let There Be Peace on Earth." And riding in his sporty red car, the three of them relished singing every tongue-twisting lyric of "Chattahoochee." Through the years, he taught them how to ride a bicycle, ski down a mountain, piece together a jigsaw puzzle, and so much more. In addition, their interests became his—whether it be soccer or saxophone, cheerleading or choir. He never missed a game, competition, or performance.

The four of us were a team. As the children grew into adults, we celebrated victories with jumps for joy, endured defeats that brought us to our knees, and sometimes rounded the bases only through giant leaps of faith. But nothing was like facing the curveball that life was about to throw our way.

CHAPTER 3

The Domino Effect

God is our refuge and strength, a very present help in trouble.
Therefore we will not fear though the earth should change,
though the mountains shake in the heart of the sea;
though its waters roar and foam,
though the mountains tremble with its tumult.

PSALM 46:1–3 RSV

With just one little push, Steve's professional life came crashing down. I suspect the dominoes had been wobbling for many months.

In early spring 2012, the law firm's managing partner urged Steve to see a doctor. Instinctively, he went to our primary care physician, who was an old friend, for a routine physical. Two weeks later, after a compulsory return visit, Steve unexpectedly came home with an order for an MRI of his brain.

I could sense a covert hand inching toward the first domino. But whose was it? And why? From behind the locked door of my bathroom, my go-to place for privacy, I called the managing partner.

"Please understand that I need to know what's going on with Steve at the firm," I implored, reminding him that Steve and I also were a partnership—his *primary* partnership.

He was extremely hesitant to share until I assured him that Steve would never know of our conversation. As he gradually began to open up, he told me several of the partners had expressed growing concerns about Steve after recent conference meetings.

"Lately, he doesn't seem to be mentally tracking our discussions," he disclosed. "Steve's participation used to be insightful, and his comments were right on the mark. Now when he speaks, it's out of context."

Clearly, they were observing someone vastly different from the brilliant attorney who for years had served on their four-person executive committee and consistently been recognized in *Who's Who in American Law, The Best Lawyers in America,* and in *Texas Monthly* as a Texas Super Lawyer. At the height of his career, Steve had written the following for the firm's website: "There is an art to law. It has to do with judgment, experience, and professionalism. This is not a bull-in-the-china-shop style of law."

There was no question that Steve possessed experience. But shockingly, his judgment and professionalism appeared to be slipping away. Understandably, his partners were worried about him, about his interactions with clients, about the potential of a future malpractice suit . . . about the possibility of Steve becoming the proverbial bull in the china shop, leaving irreparable destruction in his wake.

While this revelation grieved me, it was not entirely unexpected. For almost two years, I had wondered how long it might take for whatever was going on with Steve to affect his work. A casual phone conversation with his secretary had revealed he seldom went out to lunch with his usual group anymore, preferring instead to eat alone in his office. At home, the earliest and most obvious change had been in his ability to find the right words to express himself. While it was in Steve's DNA to live in denial about a great many things, he was keenly aware of this unexpected challenge and open with me about it. On a personal level, it was a frustrating struggle for him that resulted in halted conversation. On a professional one, it was agonizing for him to think he might not be able to deliver an impactful speech or a compelling closing argument again.

The day I sat in the neurologist's office with Steve's MRI on the wall and watched, heartbroken, as he failed to complete those few rudimentary tasks, I knew we were facing the end of his legal career and the beginning of a long, unexpected journey. Indeed, that doctor visit was the definitive push that the wobbling dominoes had awaited. The firm put him "on leave" with pay for six months to give us time to gauge our "new normal." When the six months ended, Steve would be considered permanently disabled.

There is nothing normal *about this!* every ounce of me silently screamed. *It is not a new normal! It is a terrifying and new reality!*

On Monday, April 30, 2012, Steve sprang out of bed when his alarm rang at 5:45 a.m. He showered, shaved, put in his contact lenses, blow-dried his hair, dressed in a tailor-made suit, shirt, and tie, and drove down I-30 to his law firm in Dallas—just as he had done for more than two decades. On Tuesday, May 1 (and every day thereafter for months), he arose early without an alarm, performed his morning ritual, then dressed in khaki shorts and a polo shirt and sat on the den sofa with the TV remote in one hand and a newspaper in the other.

A few weeks later, the firm invited Angela, Stephen, and me to a "retirement" party for Steve at a club in downtown Dallas. I am certain he was the youngest retiree they ever had. The evening was filled with speeches, accolades, toasts, and laugh-out-loud anecdotes highlighting his twenty-four years as a partner there. As I listened to praise upon praise being bestowed on my husband, I was filled with emotions. I was happy that the children were at last able to witness the high professional regard in which their father was held, yet deeply saddened that it was all coming to such a premature and abrupt end.

The final domino had tumbled. It was time to construct a new path.

CHAPTER 4

Deer in the Headlights

My grace is sufficient for you,
for my power is made perfect in weakness.

2 CORINTHIANS 12:9 RSV

As we faced the unknown road ahead, one thing was clear. I could not allow oncoming traffic to crush us on our journey. If there was to be a deer in the headlights, it could not be me. I determined that, with God's help, I would take the wheel. I would do everything in my power to navigate our way around any obstacles—the expected and the unexpected—for as long as I could. Not only for Steve's sake, but for Angela's and Stephen's as well.

Our next stop was the neuropsychologist's office. Hungry for any and all information, I accompanied Steve on his first visit in late May.

"The patient was referred for neuropsychological evaluation by his primary care physician to evaluate current levels of cognitive and emotional functioning," the initial report stated.

"I am having trouble with my speech," Steve confided at his appointment. The doctor agreed, describing it in writing as "effortful, choppy, and hesitant."

During the interview, however, it rapidly became evident that Steve was having greater cognitive difficulties than he openly admitted. More comprehensive testing was recommended.

A week later, Steve drove himself back to the neuropsychologist's office for a series of tests lasting several hours. Just as with the simple tasks in the neurologist's office weeks before, Steve had considerable difficulty even understanding what he was being asked to do.

"He has a kind of *deer in the headlights* look at times," the doctor wrote. It was a look I knew well—stunned, confused, paralyzed to act.

Throughout every area of testing that day, his scores were "well below expectation" and, in many cases, his performance was "severely impaired." Given Steve's educational and professional background, the doctor concluded that in all areas these were "acquired deficits," indicating significant changes in his brain.

"It is clear there is a global decline in intellectual capabilities," his report stated. *Global?* Little wonder I felt the world as we knew it was imploding!

"Personality data do not suggest any significant emotional component and I suspect that this reflects his general lack of insight into the seriousness of his cognitive problems," the neuropsychologist continued.

And finally, he wrote, "**Diagnostic Impression: 331.0 Alzheimer's Disease**."

There it was, its ugly face staring straight into ours.

CHAPTER 5

Gazing in the Rearview Mirror

Put on then, as God's chosen ones, holy and beloved,
compassion, kindness, lowliness, meekness, and patience,
forbearing one another and,
if one has a complaint against another, forgiving each other;
as the Lord has forgiven you, so you also must forgive.

COLOSSIANS 3:12–13 RSV

"The smartest man I know couldn't draw a clock!" Our son was dumbfounded. "To learn that his abilities were that limited hit me in the face. My whole idea of what my dad could do instantly changed," Stephen recalled.

Finding the right words, time, and setting to tell the children about their father's diagnosis was not easy. To this day, I doubt that I got it right.

Angela, at age twenty-two, had recently graduated from TCU and was working at a local preschool until an opportunity to teach art in the Fort Worth Independent School District arose. Stephen was a TCU student on the cusp of celebrating his twenty-first birthday and still deliberating his destiny. Because both had remained in our hometown, they had spent more time around their dad than most college students do.

"We already knew there was something off, but we couldn't put our finger on it," Angela said in hindsight. "Even before his diagnosis, it was impossible not to realize something was changing; something was quite different. We had been picking up pieces of conversation, filling in sentences for him for so long. And some of the things he had been doing were not only out of character but socially uncomfortable. I remember thinking this behavior wasn't the normal, adorable, dad-embarrassing kind, and being anxious about what he might do next."

Taking in the Alzheimer's news for the first time, Stephen questioned himself: "What did I miss? Why is this so shocking to me?"

Later he reflected, "The signs—his issues with word recall, numbers, memory, and problem-solving; his failure to respect others' personal space by standing too close in line; and the increasingly unpredictable mood swings—were all there. Everything I assumed was just a part of aging was actually Alzheimer's! Dad's diagnosis hit me really hard as I thought about his own father having lived with that terrible disease, but it also helped explain so many things."

The children had known Steve's father as having Alzheimer's in his later years . . . older than their dad was at the onset. Unfortunately, since he lived in Houston and they only saw him a few times a year, the effect of the disease was much of what they remembered of their kind, hardworking, loving grandfather.

On the other hand, we lived just around the corner from my parents, and Angela and Stephen each formed a close bond with my dad from birth. They knew him as a smart, vibrant, devoted family man who taught them good manners, important life lessons, and how to play gin rummy. As I looked at my own young adulthood in life's rearview mirror, I clearly saw the cherished relationship I'd shared with my father. I had often confided in him, and he had never failed to counsel me with insight and wisdom. How it saddened me that Angela and Stephen were already losing those opportunities with their own father! And I grieved the fact that they would never get to see him introduce his grandchildren to the music of Willie Nelson or show them how to separate out the straight-edge pieces of a jigsaw puzzle.

Together the three of us realized how Steve had compensated for his decreasing mental abilities over the years. When he relied on his cell phone to calculate the gratuity at the end of a restaurant meal, we had chastised him. "It's not that hard to figure out a fifteen or twenty percent tip," one of us would say. Now we understood. Not only was it that hard for him—it was impossible as well.

Early-onset Alzheimer's impacts not only work and family, but also finances. Blessedly, within the past year I had begun paying the monthly bills—a task Steve had dutifully performed throughout our married life. Initially, I took over the job to give him more free time . . . or at least that's what I said. On some level, I knew I needed to step in on the financial front. And thank goodness I did *when* I did! A person who can no longer do basic math certainly should not be relied on to balance a bank account.

Whereas I am technologically challenged, Steve was always the boy with the newest gadget. He perpetually embraced the ever-evolving technology of televisions, computers, and phones, desiring each new version as soon as it came on the market. If it was new or improved, he had to have it. However, he had become increasingly dependent on our kids to help him navigate this realm. The problem was they were not available 24/7, and even when they agreed to assist, he could be irritatingly impatient.

"We got so frustrated with him," Angela admitted. "I wanted him just to let some of it—some of that obsession, some of that pride—go."

Of course, he did not willingly let it go. Only later-stage dementia could take away his obsession and stubborn pride . . . along with many of the best parts of him as well.

Early reflections on the changes we had observed in Steve brought to mind a trip that he, Angela, and I had taken to New York City only a few weeks before the MRI scan of his brain. For decades, Steve had traveled to Manhattan on business, and he knew the street names and grids like a vivid mental map. We relied on him to be our trusted guide as he always had been. The moment we arrived in the city, however, it became apparent to Angela and to me that his sense of direction was fuzzy at best, and we needed to take over as guides, as well as in other ways. When he struggled to adjust the simple thermostat in the hotel room, I tried to help.

"Don't manage me!" he admonished. His ego did not want me to step in because he did not want to admit there were things he could no longer do.

Sorrow for our collective loss, shock at the depth of his limitations, yet little surprise that all the changes he was experiencing had a name . . . our reactions to Steve's diagnosis were much the same. But the ways in which we acted out our feelings in the coming weeks and years were vastly different.

When not seeking solace in friends and work, Angela journaled, found her unique and passionate voice, and encouraged me to use mine.

Stephen, as he says, was "broken" for some time, but with divine intervention he managed to put himself back together, piece by precious piece, becoming stronger in the process.

As for me, I prayed, planned, and prepared the best I knew how for whatever was coming next. I tried not to project too far into the future, but I had to make some educated guesses to protect Steve and our family. None of it was easy. Some days I screamed when I shouldn't have; some nights I sobbed, just as I should. And I began a daily life dance with my proud husband where I increasingly took the lead while allowing him to believe he was in control . . . most of the time. Some wives do that naturally; I was not one of them.

CHAPTER 6

Family Affair

For I am the Lord your God
who takes hold of your right hand and says to you,
Do not fear; I will help you.

ISAIAH 41:13 NIV

After the children, the first person I told about Steve's diagnosis was my sister. She was the original Angela for whom our daughter was named, but our family members and her childhood friends called her Angie.

How fortunate we were to grow up in a *Father Knows Best* kind of household. Like that television series from the 1950s, our family of five was headed by two loving, attentive, role-model parents. Our dad had nicknames for all three of us kids. Tall, blonde, and beautiful, Angie was the firstborn and his "Angel." Next came Jody, his only son, who became his "Partner." Lastly, I was his little "Kitten." The threads that bound us to one another were unbreakable, as we were "knit together in love" (Colossians 2:2). Our grandparents even lived next door!

As children, we walked to our elementary school at the end of the street, worshipped in the family pew at church, played kick the can after dark with the neighborhood kids in the summer, and were typically well-behaved, as was expected. If there were problems in the world, in our city, or even in our own family, I generally was blissfully unaware. Even when my father told me, "Life isn't fair," the lesson bewildered me.

In those days, I lived in an insulated bubble. While it provided protection and stability in my youth, it also obscured my view. Eventually, it burst, as bubbles always do.

Never did I feel more exposed than when Steve's diagnosis became official. And never did Daddy's lesson about life and fairness ring more true. Now I was seeing an immensely different future than the one I had envisioned for Steve, our children, and myself. I sensed some of it would be ugly. I prayed there would be glimpses of beauty. Above all, I knew we could not face it alone. The Lord took hold of my right hand and guided me to call my sister.

"How's the packing going?" I asked Angie over the phone in May 2012.

She and her husband, Butch, were preparing to move back to Fort Worth after twenty-three years in McLean, Virginia. Both had just retired from long, successful careers there, and powerful ties were pulling them back to Texas.

For one, their daughter, Chandler, who had recently graduated from TCU and landed a good job in the Dallas–Fort Worth area, had no intention of returning to Virginia. Chandler is only six months older than our daughter, Angela, and although they grew up 1,300 miles apart, they have always called each other "sister-cousin."

For another, our parents, aged eighty-nine and ninety-one, were in exceedingly poor health and still living in our childhood home with round-the-clock care. Dad's eyesight had been failing for decades, eventually leaving him totally blind, and he was now enduring the progression of late-onset Parkinson's disease and other health issues. In spite of it all, he was the most optimistic and courageous man I ever have known. Mom was already concerned about her memory when she fell and broke her hip in 2007. I remember following the ambulance and thinking, "Life will never be the same again." And it wasn't. Not only did she never fully recover physically from the surgery, but she also rapidly declined mentally. (Had I known then that general anesthesia can hasten dementia, especially in the elderly, I would have asked the anesthesiologist about other options prior to her surgery.)

Daytime in-home care began—in a home my mother failed to recognize as her own, even though she and my father had lived there for almost sixty years. After repeated efforts to reassure her, remind her, and point out the myriad details that made it quite certainly her house, we eventually realized that the "home" she was talking about was another place altogether. The home she was remembering was the home of her childhood—something we later learned is very common.

Initially, Jody and I, who both lived nearby, divided the essential responsibilities. One or both of us visited them daily.

Through the years, we watched our precious mother decline. When she would gently pat my hand and inquire, "How are *your* parents?" it tore at my gut, and I tried not to cry. Every time she mistook Jody for our father or for her brother, it grieved him a little more. And each evening before dinner, as I watched her routinely apply eyebrow pencil and lipstick to make herself look pretty for Daddy, I knew once again she'd forgotten he was blind.

Whenever they were hospitalized, Jody and I alternated twelve-hour shifts at their bedsides, never leaving them alone. Ultimately, as both their needs increased, we transitioned to round-the-clock in-home care.

Knowing the strain we were under, Angie was drawn back to Fort Worth to help ease our load. Now, I was hesitant to unload even more bad news on her. But never will I forget what she said when I told her about Steve's diagnosis on that phone call.

Without hesitation, she announced, "If we weren't coming already, we'd be coming now!"

I knew she meant it. And God only knew how much I would need her by my side in the weeks, months, and years ahead.

CHAPTER 7

Diving In

For the Spirit God gave us does not make us timid,
but gives us power, love and self-discipline.

2 TIMOTHY 1:7 NIV

As Steve's primary caregiver, I could not just dip my toe in these new Alzheimer's waters. Only by diving in headfirst could I keep us afloat.

Early on, Steve and I met with one of his law partners to update our wills and to create durable powers of attorney and medical powers of attorney. Not surprisingly, with Steve's "lack of insight into the seriousness of his cognitive problems," it did not go as I had planned.

He insisted that if I have *his* durable and medical powers of attorney, then he should have *mine*. Did that make any sense when he had a progressive, degenerative brain disease? Absolutely not.

To keep the peace, I did the dance of letting him believe he was in control. We added the provision that Jody be named "successor agent" if either of us became incapacitated or disabled, which obviously Steve already was.

The attorney, his friend who was keenly aware of Steve's condition, did his own version of the dance by tiptoeing around the issue entirely. He never even mentioned the disease.

Steve was our family's breadwinner. While I had continued to do freelance writing and public relations work from time to time, it was solely his income that enabled our family's comfortable lifestyle. Because of this and his business education, he had always managed our financial assets and investments. Now it was vital to me that we quickly consolidate them with a financial planner whom we could trust and rely on. Thankfully, Steve readily agreed.

Within a few weeks, we selected an advisor in Houston who had been extremely helpful to Steve's father. Not only was she extraordinarily intelligent and honest, but she was also kind and compassionate when I privately divulged Steve's diagnosis. When she promised we would move through this journey together, I felt one of the many burdens that had suddenly fallen onto my shoulders being gently lifted.

Although the titles to the house and cars were in both our names, the basic utilities, along with the phone, internet, and television provider, were in Steve's name alone. Mostly, this only became an issue when there was a problem that needed to be resolved or a change that needed to be made.

Through the years, I had become accustomed to customer

service representatives telling me over the phone, "I am not authorized to talk to you about this account. Is Mr. Goodwin at home? I must have his permission to speak with you."

Now that the full responsibility for keeping our home running as smoothly as possible was mine, this annoying routine became an irritating ordeal. Nevertheless, I took the plunge and called the utility company regarding a bill.

"You will need to put Mr. Goodwin on the line to give me permission to speak with you," the representative predictably said.

"Can you come talk to this woman on the phone please?" I asked Steve, who heaved an exasperated sigh over the interruption to his TV show. As I handed him the landline receiver, I could hear the voice on the other end.

"Who am I speaking with?" she asked.

"Steve Goodwin," he answered.

"And what is your date of birth?"

His breathing became anxious as he sought out a birthday that was lost from his mind.

"And what is your date of birth?" she repeated.

I whispered the correct date to him. But just as I could hear the customer service rep's voice, she unfortunately could hear mine.

"Ma'am," she scolded, "you are not allowed to give him the answers."

If I was not allowed to give my husband the answers he needed, then who was? Wasn't I a customer too? This clearly was not going to work. I had to jump through and around hoops to secure even the simplest of customer services. More than once, I strategically placed a call while Stephen was at home. After all, he too was "Mr. Goodwin," and he could supply an essential male voice. Even though I was always acting on Steve's behalf—on *our* behalf—it never ceased to be incredibly frustrating. There just had to be a better way.

Through the years, as Angela and Stephen moved toward adulthood, Steve often would lovingly ask me, "What can we do for the kids?"

My reply was always, "Take care of ourselves so they don't have to worry about us!"

For too long, I had witnessed the financial burden that twenty-four-hour care placed on my elderly parents without the assistance of long-term care insurance. I never wanted the two of us to be in a similar situation. Yet every time I brought up the subject of long-term care policies, Steve responded, "Maybe later, after we've finished paying college tuition."

Unfortunately, we didn't get to that "later" soon enough. Stephen was still a TCU student when Steve received his Alzheimer's diagnosis, which rendered him ineligible for long-term care insurance. For myself, I purchased a policy as quickly as I could after that.

Medically, of course, I wanted to seek out the best for Steve. Alzheimer's has no cure; I was not looking for one. But because of my mother's struggles with dementia, I knew there were a few prescription drugs believed to temporarily improve symptoms. The neurologist who had been treating both my parents agreed to see Steve. She had a good bedside manner. Nevertheless, at first, she was almost as befuddled as the neurologist who had initially viewed his MRI.

"Can you drive?" she asked him.

"I can drive to Oklahoma today if I want to," he responded. To me, that was just one of many frightening possibilities in a list that was growing daily.

Next she thought perhaps frontotemporal dementia was the culprit.

"Can you name all the parts of your watch?" she inquired, pointing at his left wrist.

"Yes," he responded. But as she touched the watchband, face, and stem, he failed to name any of them.

I desperately wanted to speak with her alone as, given Steve's denial, it was excruciatingly uncomfortable talking about him while he was in the room. Then I had an idea.

"Honey, would you mind sitting in the waiting room for just a little while?" I asked Steve. "I'd like to talk to the doctor about my parents for a few minutes. You'll be more comfortable there. I promise I'll be out soon, and then we'll go grab lunch."

It worked. As I told the neurologist more about Steve's symptoms, she eventually agreed with his Alzheimer's diagnosis. She added two new medications to his daily routine, and I began arranging his pills in a weekly organizer to help both of us keep track.

Soon I taped a large, color-coded, monthly calendar—like the one we had used for the children's school and extracurricular activities—back on the refrigerator. I hoped it would be a visual reminder to Steve not only of the current month and the days of the week but also of holidays, social engagements, doctors' appointments, TCU sporting events, and the like.

Around this same time, Angie and Butch were getting settled in Fort Worth and often expressed their desire to help us in any way.

Butch arranged for me to meet with his good friend whose husband had died from complications of Alzheimer's at the age of sixty-one—the exact age Steve was now.

Before his death, they had been active as a couple in support groups and brain health studies in their Dallas community. Considering Steve's level of denial, I predicted those kinds of engagements would not work for the two of us. She understood. In fact, she is the first person who told me, "If you've seen one Alzheimer's patient, you've seen one." As she explained, "This is not a one-approach-fits-all disease, but there are many things we all have in common."

When I asked for her advice, she encouraged our family to take full advantage of this open window of opportunity to share experiences with Steve while he could still enjoy them . . . just as she and her family had done. Those words stuck with me.

She also wisely suggested I seek out the Alzheimer's Association and all its resources, which I promptly did.

At our local Alzheimer's Association office, I met with the social worker, who was both empathetic and emphatic. She patiently listened and gave me some informational materials and a list of suggested books.

Additionally, she urged me to contact the Social Security Administration regarding disability benefits as soon as possible. Her strong recommendation was to make a face-to-face appointment, taking Steve and all documentation of his dementia along. This proved to be excellent advice as the representative could see firsthand that Steve was cognitively impaired and therefore moved the process along accordingly.

In life, we are forced to learn a multitude of lessons, occasionally about things we never really wanted to know about. The copious amounts of required paperwork regarding Steve's disease and disabilities fall into that category. And the Social Security forms were but one chore in a long list.

So you would think I'd have known better. Answering question after question with pen in hand as I sat at the dining room table, I called Steve in from the den where he was watching television as usual.

"Can you make change for a dollar?" I asked him. It was one of the questions on the form.

"What?" he responded in a huff.

"Can you make change for a dollar?" I repeated.

Of course he couldn't, and he knew it. I think I knew it too. He grabbed a handful of change from his pocket and slammed it down hard on the table in front of me.

"There!" he exclaimed, stomping angrily back to his chair.

The indentations on the dining table remained long after the coins were removed and the form was completed. They were a permanent, painful reminder of my carelessness that day. Why did I need to ask that question—or any question—when ninety-nine percent of me already knew the answer?

Thankfully, Steve was approved for disability shortly thereafter with no appeal necessary. It sounds odd to say that receiving early Social Security and Medicare benefits can be a boost not only to your bank account but also to your morale. But given our here-and-now circumstances, it was.

We were grateful for another boost too. Although Steve had no long-term care insurance, he had wisely purchased two valuable disability policies through the law firm many years prior. Not until he was placed "on leave" at the firm was I even aware the policies existed.

After several lengthy conversations with the assigned insurance agent, I completed more mounds of paperwork, sent documentation of Steve's diagnosis along with a copy of his power of attorney, and soon gratefully deposited the first benefits check. One policy would end when Steve turned sixty-seven, the other, larger one at age seventy.

Nine years later—three weeks after Steve's seventieth birthday—a newly assigned disability claims specialist informed me that the larger policy actually contained a lifetime security benefit. Because of Steve's "severe cognitive impairment," it would continue to pay until his death. The Lord had given us a gift I had not even known to ask for.

We were checking items off the practical side of our list. But what about the emotional side? And where could I find guidance as we journeyed along this road? The social worker referred me to a long-running Alzheimer's caregiver support group to help meet those needs. I would get there soon enough . . .

But there was something we needed to do first. As I stood before our family's "open window of opportunity," I could feel a come-and-get-it breeze.

CHAPTER 8

Diminishing Breezes, Shifting Winds

*I am with you and will watch over you wherever you go,
and I will bring you back to this land.
I will not leave you until I have done what I have promised you.*

GENESIS 28:15 NIV

How our foursome loved family vacations! We treasure our funny photo of Stephen with Old Faithful seemingly erupting out of the back of his head and the one of him savoring high tea at the fancy Empress Hotel in Victoria. We hold sweet memories of Angela, dressed head to toe in pink denim astride her favorite horse at a Colorado dude ranch, as well as bittersweet ones of her leaving her cherished teddy bear on a Florida beach.

Given Steve's diagnosis, the idea of putting off any family trips for the future quickly became impractical. While traveling was a financial stretch in our new reality, the pull was strong and, in many ways, I felt we couldn't afford *not* to go. With Angie and Jody readily agreeing to assume my caregiving responsibilities for our parents, now was the time to use all those stockpiled frequent flier miles. We were going to follow the inviting breeze and have all the fun we could before the window closed for good. And although I had never been dutiful about compiling photo albums or scrapbooks, a nudge from above told me to preserve these memories in the making. I am so glad I did.

The first breeze we caught in the summer of 2012 was a glacial one—on a long-hoped-for Alaskan cruise. All in all, it went well. Angela and Stephen were patiently discovering how best to relate to and respond to their dad. As a bonus, I was learning from their interactions. Prior to the cruise, the kids and I had carefully endeavored to select shore excursions their father would be able to participate in and enjoy with us. Yes, Steve had to frantically search for his identification card to reboard the ship after a couple of those excursions. And no, he could not follow the guide's paddling instructions on our whitewater rafting adventure, even though that was an activity we had delighted in on several previous vacations. Still, the overall experience emboldened us to travel even farther the next summer.

That is when the breeze beckoned from off the Mediterranean, bringing us to Italy. With the help of a dear travel agent friend, I found a fabulous group tour that took us through the Lake Country, Venice, Florence, and Rome. Best of all, we wouldn't have to do any planning ourselves! Just stick to the itinerary and enjoy. With the exception of a few free afternoons, everything was scheduled for us.

Often, the camera caught Steve smiling—at the beautiful villa on Lake Como, in a gondola in picturesque Venice, eating luscious pizza in Sienna. Yet the trip had its challenges as well. While he seemed to genuinely enjoy the museums, churches, and walking tours (sometimes outpacing even our guide!), he became aggravated and impatient when we wanted to browse the charming shops. On several occasions, we had to redirect him into our assigned row on the bus. And although the excessive heat in Rome affected us all, it seemed to oppress Steve more than most.

Worst of all, one evening in Florence at a restaurant with the rest of our tour group, he became visibly and audibly agitated over a three-course Italian menu, which we were trying to help him understand. Each course—appetizer, entrée, and dessert—had a selection of three items from which we could order one per course. When Steve saw something he liked on the menu, he wanted to order it—even if it was three appetizers and two entrées. We tried to explain. We tried to compromise. We tried to intercede with the server. But Steve wasn't having any of that.

"I want what I want!" he proclaimed, and he didn't care who heard him.

On the final night of our trip, the father of another family on the tour discreetly pulled Stephen aside. "I want you to know that I see what you are doing for your family," he acknowledged. Surely, it would have been impossible to spend ten days with us and not notice that something was off with Steve and that the kids were stepping in and helping out in extraordinary ways. Although they certainly weren't doing it for praise, those few words of affirmation refueled their emotional tanks and helped to keep us going.

The window was clearly closing, but the next summer we could still feel the hint of a breeze. This time, it was tropical. We decided on a Hawaiian vacation after Stephen wisely nixed my overly ambitious idea of a tour through France.

"Mom! Dad has enough trouble with our own language, much less a foreign one," he reminded me. "Please, please let's go somewhere they speak English!"

He was right. That recommendation led to the last big trip our foursome would ever take—one that was hands down Steve's favorite. After he purchased enough Hawaiian shirts for a lifetime and Stephen assisted him in packing every single one, we flew to Honolulu and then on to Maui.

For the most part, our days and nights were welcomely unstructured. Our hotel was on a gorgeous beach, and we could enjoy all the sand, surf, and sun we desired. Steve loved seafood. In Maui, it was fresh and abundant on every menu. If he could not decide which fish to order, we all would order different entrées and share. Cocktails and mocktails wore orchids and umbrellas. We wore swimsuits and sunscreen. Thanks to Angela and Stephen helping me to buffer against any foreseeable obstacles, we experienced much more pleasure than pressure during our time in Hawaii.

Flying with Steve on airplanes, however, had become increasingly difficult. TSA regulations inconvenience everyone, but they are especially trying for those with dementia. Before we ever reached the first security line, we attempted a discussion with Steve about why he could not have a pocketknife in his carry-on bag. He seemed to have forgotten all about the events and aftermath of 9/11.

Arguing ensued, but it was nothing compared to what might have happened in a confrontation with a TSA agent. Eventually, in loud exasperation, Steve slammed the knife into the trash can. Once we arrived at screening, we made certain he was flanked on both sides. One of us went ahead in case Steve was uncooperative and we needed to de-escalate the situation by explaining his disease to the agent. Another followed to help him get his keys, wallet, and cell phone into the bowl, and his shoes and carry-on onto the belt. And, oh, that carry-on! What had been my practical, pre-Alzheimer's gift to him was worse than useless now. There were way too many compartments, pockets, zippers, buckles, and hiding places inviting a disorganized mind to lose an ID and boarding pass.

Nevertheless, we were ultimately gratified we made the trip. When we returned home and Angie asked Steve what he had enjoyed most, he grinned and enthusiastically replied, "Everything!"

However brave or foolish, I determined that the two of us would embark on several more trips. Fearing Steve would soon lose the opportunity to visit his family members, I made seeing them a priority.

In September, we flew to Destin, Florida, to spend a few days with his cousin and her family. As an only child, she had always cherished her relationship with Steve and his brother, Phil. It was good to catch up, meet her newest grandchildren, cruise the water on her husband's boat, and once again eat fresh, delicious seafood. It was *not* good when Steve got frustrated with my momentary lack of direction and speedily wandered away on the Destin Harbor Boardwalk. In fact, it was terrifying! With my heart pounding, I begged him to never do that again. We were soon headed to New York City, and I did not want him to get lost in Times Square . . . or anywhere.

Our visit to Manhattan presented a perfect opportunity to see Steve's second cousins, Norma and Dave. As a boy, Steve's paternal grandfather had run away from his English home and family on a ship destined for the States. Rummaging through a box of old letters in the attic in the 1990s, Steve's father was delighted to discover correspondence from long-lost cousins in Suffolk. Sadly, most of that generation had passed on, but fortunately, he had been able to connect by mail with Norma and Dave. Steve and I had visited them in their home by the North Sea and had also welcomed them to our home. Given where we were on Steve's Alzheimer's journey, I was fairly certain we would not be traveling abroad again. So when Norma told me they would be ending a New England fall foliage tour in New York City, I leaped at our chance to meet them there. Together, the four of us dined in Tribeca, took an emotional tour of the 9/11 Memorial, and made the long hike through Central Park to Strawberry Fields. Steve was still the fastest walker of us all.

After those trips, however, I realized I could no longer bear sole responsibility for him when we traveled.

The next time Steve and I ventured back to Manhattan was with Mary Claire, my dear friend since college, to see her son Ben perform in his own original musical theater production. It was a one-night-only opportunity in January 2015, and a very special three days in the city. Knowing our Alzheimer's struggles well, Mary Claire provided a calming, encouraging, and intuitive presence throughout. Fortunately, Steve got lost only in the enormity of Ben's talent and in the irresistible music of *Beautiful: The Carole King Musical* on Broadway.

In May, Stephen accompanied us to Santa Fe, one of Steve's favorite destinations that he had long desired to share with our son. Having someone there to help with Steve at the airport and in navigating new situations was now crucial, and Stephen had gotten good at it. As long as we were doing what Steve wanted to do in the moment, he was happy—whether visiting the art galleries, getting Stephen fitted for a new cowboy hat, or sitting on a rooftop deck. After giving our guide a confidential heads-up regarding Steve's condition, the three of us were even able to enjoy a trail ride in the mountains on horseback. Blessedly, that risk was worth the reward.

Because of the disease progression, however, our final two trips were considerably riskier. Never one to say no to my sister, against my better judgment I agreed we would join her and Butch's family on a Caribbean cruise in the summer of 2015. Thankfully, Steve stopped short of yelling, "Get me off this thing!" and trying to jump ship. But in this larger group setting, it was not always possible to do precisely what Steve wanted to do at the exact moment he wanted to do it. Fearing he would get lost, I made certain we all stuck together. He was stubborn. He was impatient. There were outbursts, including forcibly smashing his drink onto the deck.

"What's wrong with Uncle Steve?" our young great-nieces and great-nephews began to ask on board the ship.

"You know how bad you feel when you're sick with a stomach-ache?" I responded. "Your Uncle Steve is sick in his brain . . . and there isn't any medicine that can make him well."

I hope that helped them understand a bit. Any further explanation I left to their parents.

That winter, along with Stephen, Angela, and her boyfriend-turned-fiancé, Matt, Steve and I attended a close friend's wedding in Maryland. Shaken by their father's uncharacteristic and unpredictable behaviors—such as his thwarted attempt to drink wine straight from the bottle at the reception—the kids and I were unshaken in our agreement thereafter that the window of opportunity had firmly closed.

The winds were shifting mightily.

CHAPTER 9

The Case of the Missing Casseroles

Praise be to the God and Father of our Lord Jesus Christ,
the Father of compassion and the God of all comfort,
who comforts us in all our troubles,
so that we can comfort those in any trouble
with the comfort we ourselves receive from God.

2 CORINTHIANS 1:3–4 NIV

In Texas and across the South, when someone falls ill or a family member dies, friends bring you food. That's how we express our love. If you have the flu, they bring hearty chicken soup. If you are mourning a death, they bring rich, creamy casseroles along with heavenly cakes and pies. If you are recovering from surgery, they bring delicious dinners designed to build you back up. Chicken and dumplings. Macaroni and cheese. Comfort food.

That doesn't happen when you have Alzheimer's disease. Friends don't know what to do. Even though your brain is actively dying, you do not look sick—at least not for a very long time.

In 2012, several months after telling close family about Steve's diagnosis, I began to confide in a few of our dearest friends despite his objections and without his knowledge. Never did I regret that decision. My motives were pure. Not only did I want them to understand why his vocabulary, memory, and behaviors were changing, but I also knew deep down we would need all the support we could muster on this journey. If knowledge is power, their knowledge about Steve's disease empowered these friends to become more patient, compassionate, and forgiving when they were with him. It helped them to help us both. Nevertheless, as I wrote in my journal, opening up was not easy.

> If I am honest with others about where my life is and what I am feeling, I sense that I am bringing everyone down and that they assume I am seeking their pity.
>
> If I don't disclose Steve's diagnosis and our new reality—which changes often and without notice—I feel I am being fake. I feel not that I am rising above and becoming more than myself, but rather, that I am somehow being less than my whole self.
>
> Yet I wonder: Why burden them? I know that some will keep it in their hearts and remember. Others will offer kind words and forget. The former are surely truer friends than the latter. And the ones who figure out how to help are the truest, best friends of all.

But it is still a burden I am asking them to bear with us. I never dreamed this would be our load—and one I would need help carrying.

Not everyone is lucky enough to have a support system like ours. Sometimes, after a diagnosis of dementia, people you once thought were friends simply vanish from your life. That didn't happen to us. Although our friends have been universally sympathetic, their initial reactions varied from affirmation to bewilderment to disbelief—the latter of which no doubt was based on a misperception of Steve rather than our day-to-day reality.

Initially, one confidante thought Steve's apparent dementia stemmed from hearing loss, so she brought me numerous scientific references on the connection between the two. Indeed, his hearing loss was as real as his denial of it. For years, he had played the stereo system and television at deafening levels. But truly, that concern was now only a whisper in our discordant new reality. Although a hearing aid might have helped a bit if Steve had been willing to wear one, we were significantly past the point of such a device providing the kind of aid he most needed.

Another friend lectured and questioned me at length as to whether Steve's dementia was in fact Alzheimer's disease. I tried to listen patiently. I tried not to interrupt. I tried to imagine what possible positive outcome he hoped his words would produce. But the truth hung over our family like a massive highway sign. Even though we were still early in our journey, I knew the name of the road we were on.

After giving themselves a little time to wrap their minds around what truly was happening inside Steve's brain, these two friends, as well as others with whom I'd shared Steve's diagnosis and many who had heard the news through the grapevine, demonstrated their support in remarkably caring and generous ways.

One of Steve's pals and admirers frequently visited our home, where he would share his ideas for new inventions and revisit treasured memories over a glass of carefully selected red wine. Numerous couple friends invited us out to dinner, picked us up in their car, and politely insisted on paying our bill . . . time and time again. One chartered a small plane and generously flew us and another couple to their new beach house for a long weekend. I never knew if they could hear Steve's rising frustration through the bedroom walls of that splendid house as I pleaded with him to keep his voice down. If they did, they were kind enough to not mention it.

On occasion, a few of Steve's best buddies picked him up for lunch at a favorite restaurant, which he always looked forward to and enjoyed. It didn't take long for them to learn to schedule these outings through me, however, as Steve's sense of time became more and more confused. Fellow attorneys thoughtfully took him to meetings of the Inn of Court, an organization that Steve was immensely proud to be a member of. They even graciously made sure that one of its highest honors was bestowed on Steve "sooner rather than later," while he was still able to attend the ceremony and value its significance.

Girlfriends rallied around me with frequent phone calls and an occasional girls' night out. They prayed for us. Offering me continued words of encouragement, Mary Claire often affirmed, "You're doing great!"

In June 2014, the year we turned sixty, a close group of TCU sorority sisters and I took a weekend trip to New Orleans to celebrate. It was my first girls' trip ever, and it was long overdue. We had so much fun that the next summer, we spent four glorious nights in La Jolla, where one of our group owned a condo. In the twelve intervening months, however, things had changed enough with Steve that I was no longer comfortable with the idea of leaving him alone both day and night. Angela and Stephen readily agreed to take turns spending the evenings and nights with their dad so that I could go. They knew I needed some time away. But when my girlfriends began planning a four-day trip to San Francisco for July 2016, I told the group I wouldn't be able to join. I just couldn't be that far away from Steve for that long.

Over those months and years, our time spent with friends became less of a conversation *with* Steve and more of a conversation *around* him. He would blurt sentences out of context. He might incessantly repeat or interrupt. He would become the deer in the headlights.

This became strikingly clear during college football season. Stephen and his roommates enjoyed hosting "tailgate" type parties before TCU games at their house, which was within walking distance of the stadium. They always invited a few friends and were kind to include Steve and me as well. After we said our goodbyes to the group on a warm autumn afternoon, one of Stephen's friends, who had not seen Steve in several years, approached our son.

"Man, your dad was wasted!" the friend said.

Of course, he wasn't. Steve was suffering the effects of Alzheimer's, not alcohol. But it reminded me again why I had felt compelled to share his diagnosis with our own friends.

Even so, dining out with them presented more and more of a challenge. Navigating menus became overwhelming for Steve, so I ordered for him. If his preferred grilled salmon was not available, I offered him two choices. Often, he fumbled with the proper dining utensils and sometimes forgot his manners. While the rest of us were relaxing and enjoying the evening, he acted anxious to leave. Despite all the changes, our wonderful friends stuck with us month after month, year after year.

Eventually, when making simple small talk and remembering names became impossible, Steve compensated with an expressive new way of greeting: an enormous (though often surprising) bear hug, an ingratiating smile, and a voice spilling over with enthusiasm as he asked, "How's the family?" It was his temporary new love language.

CHAPTER 10

Small Victories

I will instruct you and teach you in the way you should go;
I will counsel you with my loving eye on you.

PSALM 32:8 NIV

As the Lord gave me comfort through friends and sent me strength through family, he subsequently provided instructional and emotional guidance through a brand-new source.

Enter the caregiver support group, sponsored by our local chapter of the Alzheimer's Association. It met for two hours in the morning on the first and third Thursdays of every month. Luckily, it was easy to find; it met at our church. Everyone there, facilitator and participant alike, was united against a common enemy: progressive dementia. Although we all realized that none of us could win the war, each of us discovered that, with help, we could achieve small victories. That is what kept us coming back every two weeks and what kept us going while caring for our loved ones.

The association also sponsored a support group tailored for people in the early stages of dementia. When I suggested to Steve that he take part in one of those, he replied in his usual manner—"Not yet." I knew that meant never.

I also knew that he was extremely sensitive to any mention of his struggles with Alzheimer's. Always it was the elephant in the room. He did not want me discussing it with family, friends, or even doctors, and certainly not with strangers. So my participating in the caregiver support group was going to be a hard sell. Then an idea came to me as it had in the neurologist's office . . . I told him I was attending for advice on how to help my mother as she battled vascular dementia. He was fine with that, provided I always return in time to accompany him to lunch.

Once I joined the group, I took notes and tried to absorb all the information I could. Some participants had been on this journey with their loved ones for many years; others were just beginning. Because of my experience with my precious mom, I was somewhere in the middle.

Recently, Angie, Jody, and I had found that not only was it acceptable but also often preferable to sometimes skirt around the truth with Mom. When she first began to ask repeatedly about her deceased mother, time and again we had answered, "She is in heaven." Then we learned "She's delayed in traffic" or "She's at the store and will be here soon" were far better answers. They satisfied her for the moment, did not make her sad, and the subject was quickly forgotten until the next time when we would do it all over again.

Did these responses run contrary to everything our parents taught us about truth and honesty? Of course. Were they the right things to say? Absolutely. We gave ourselves permission to leave our world and enter hers. The Alzheimer's Association has a wonderful name for this: *fiblet*, a kind of therapeutic lie. And it came up in the support group often.

As the newcomer to the group, I listened to the others' stories . . .

One elderly man, who had worked hard and saved carefully all his life, was distraught about applying for Medicaid because his wife's care was depleting their finances.

Another man always left our meeting ten minutes early in order to arrive on time for a daily lunch with his wife, who lived at a nearby memory care facility.

Also new to the group was the young woman at odds with her family over guardianship, money, and what ultimately would be best for her father, who was in the early stages of dementia.

For another member, the support group was a continuing social connection and an opportunity to pay it forward as his wife had died of complications from Alzheimer's several months earlier.

Perhaps the story that hit closest to home was told by a woman who felt tremendous guilt about placing her husband, who could still play the piano with finesse but struggled in other ways, in memory care. While Steve's talents were far different and we were years away from transitioning to a facility, the difficulties she spoke of in dealing with her partner's behavioral changes at home and her conflicted feelings about moving him struck a chord.

The group is where I first heard about the "four magic distractions"—children, music, sweets, and animals—the few things that individuals with dementia typically enjoy up until the final stages of the disease.

Although at this time in our lives we were around children infrequently, Steve found happiness in the presence of our great-nieces and great-nephews, as well as in waving and making funny faces at babies and toddlers in restaurants and stores—much to Angela's and Stephen's embarrassment.

His love of all kinds of music in its many forms continued until it was overtaken by his attraction to movies and sports on television for a while. Later, it returned with an unexpected, happy twist.

In the earlier stages, sweets were not much of a temptation for Steve. He would have eaten salmon and spinach at every meal if available—perhaps allowing himself a couple of chocolate chip cookies as a midday snack. No way his Alzheimer's was brought on by lifestyle! Later in the progression, however, ice cream, pie, cake, and all manner of sweets gave him pleasure.

And then there were animals. Steve had yearned for another dog ever since our beloved golden retriever passed away at the age of fifteen. I kept delaying, as I felt we were fine empty nesters without one. He also had harped on his desire for a new bicycle "for exercise," as he said. Along with his physician, I repeatedly discouraged that idea as well, fearing the increasing odds of him getting lost or having a terrible accident.

Finally, after yet another visit to the doctor, I acquiesced. "If you will stop talking about getting a bike, we will get a dog. And you can walk the dog—for exercise!"

Thus began our search for a new canine companion. Steve wasn't particular about the age or the breed, provided it was of the larger variety. Foreseeing my growing responsibilities at home, I did not want a puppy to house-train, wrestle shoes from, or teach how to walk on a leash. My initial attempts at adopting an older golden retriever from a rescue organization were unsuccessful.

Finally, after several weeks on the internet, I found Nora, an eleven-month-old, shaggy, taupe labradoodle with golden eyes. Her owners were selling her because they'd become overwhelmed with a three-year-old son, another child on the way, and a back-yard with no fence. Nora was good-natured and well cared for, with enough energy to power a rocket ship.

For Steve, it was love at first sight.

For Stephen, it was "Mom, have you lost your mind?"

Indeed, Nora did not pee on the rug or chew on Steve's sneak-ers, but otherwise she was not well trained. In group classes at the local pet store, she was banished to "time-out" in the corner because she was too social with the other dogs. Subsequently, we paid a trainer to come to our house, where we worked on "Sit," "Stay," and "Don't run out the front door!" When I sensed the train-er's frustration with Steve's inability to understand the proper cues, I realized I should have told her about his dementia at the outset. Once I did, she softened and saw that Nora was able to learn new things although, sadly, her primary owner was not.

Ironically, the dog we got "for exercise" never did learn how to walk properly on a leash. But she did become Steve's constant companion and, along the way, my unexpected ally.

In support group, whenever the subject of driving came up, I lis-tened with extra attention, absorbing every possible scenario. As the facilitator advised, none of us wanted our family member to get lost, cause an accident, or, worse yet, injure someone and be sued for driving with dementia. Better to be proactive than made to react to a tragic event that could have been avoided.

When it came to dealing with this touchy subject, every family's story was different. One husband willingly gave up driving after getting lost on his way home. Another continually looked for his car keys that his wife had carefully hidden. A father in the earlier stages of dementia agreed to stop driving at night and only drove on certain streets during the day.

Somehow, I knew none of that would work for us. Once again, when the time was right, we would need to find our own path. That path began opening up one afternoon when Steve returned from our neighborhood gas station almost as quickly as he left. He was visibly upset.

"They want all these numbers! Lots of numbers!" he repeated in exasperation.

I had to mentally picture myself at the gas pump to discern what he was talking about . . . Oh, the zip code! Although Steve was still able to drive to the station, pull up to the pump, and insert his credit card, he was unable to enter our zip code. I am not sure whether he simply could not remember the numbers or whether he no longer understood what a zip code meant.

"That's okay, honey," I said in an effort to reassure him. "Let me ride with you and we'll figure it out together."

After we filled up his car, I wrote our zip code on a slip of paper that I placed in his glove compartment. He was grateful but soon forgot it was there.

As he drove us home, I delicately suggested, "Steve, if you aren't able to put gas in your car, maybe you should stop driving." He looked at me as though I was the one losing brain cells.

Thereafter, I accompanied him whenever he wanted to run an errand to the dry cleaners or to the drugstore (where instead of buying one shampoo or deodorant at a time, he now put five of each in the cart). On our way to the cleaners one afternoon, he rolled through a stop sign. Then he drove past all the streets we typically might take. For a while, I said nothing, thinking he would eventually turn in the right direction. But he didn't. It was clear he had forgotten how to get there.

The next day, I wrote and delivered a confidential note to Steve's physician requesting that he tell my husband he could no longer drive. For this effort to be successful, I knew the conversation must be initiated by someone other than me—someone who could speak to him not only doctor-to-patient, but also doctor-to-lawyer, man-to-man, friend-to-friend.

"Are you still driving, Steve?" the doctor asked during his appointment.

"Yes," he replied.

"Well, you shouldn't. When you do, it's like driving after drinking a six-pack of beer. Not a good idea."

"But I *can* drive!" Steve argued.

"I know," the doctor responded firmly, "but I am telling you that you shouldn't."

For the most part, that simple, direct conversation worked for us.

Since then, I've learned that some physicians write a "No Driving" prescription for the dementia patient, which can help in several ways. It may serve as a visual reminder, assist with subsequent changes in auto insurance premiums, or aid when switching from a driver's license to an ID card.

One thing is certain, however. When the time is right, whatever way the individual's driving eventually comes to an end—so long as it is without accident, injury, or becoming lost far from home—it is a not-so-small victory.

In the support group, managing challenging behaviors was another frequent topic. We discussed behaviors ranging from compulsive hoarding to irrational fears to extreme combativeness and every-thing else imaginable. I learned to use fiblets. I learned to redirect. And I learned, in Steve's angriest moments, to physically back away and even retreat into my bathroom behind a locked door. It was a lesson I tucked away for the future.

CHAPTER 11

Keel and Anchor

When you pass through the waters, I will be with you;
and when you pass through the rivers,
they will not sweep over you.

ISAIAH 43:2 NIV

If I was the keel that held our family ship together, Steve had been the anchor that kept us from drifting too far in any storm. Now that our anchor was being ripped from its depths, we'd surely face some rough seas ahead.

In 2012, when Steve received his diagnosis, Angela, thankfully, was in a good place in her life. She had endured some unimaginably difficult years in high school, and with help, hard work, and God's grace, she had emerged with a healthy sense of self-worth and an optimistic view of her future. "My person" is how she referred to her dad, and they shared a unique and unbreakable bond. Whenever I got too involved in the myriad details of her daily life, which I often did as her mother, Steve could be relied on to step back and see the big picture. Angela valued his wisdom and advice. Now she had a college degree, a full-time job, and a wonderful, steady boyfriend in Matt, her future husband.

Stephen's story around this time, however, was a bit more complicated. He was a junior in college in 2012, and his university experience was not going at all as he had imagined. After suffering two season-ending football injuries in high school, he was overjoyed to be an "invited walk-on" placekicker entering his freshman year at TCU. A summer bout with mononucleosis that prevented him from working out with the team and a strained muscle before tryouts, unfortunately, were the handwriting on the locker room wall. He did not make the team. And he was stuck in the mire of disappointment, struggling both emotionally and academically for a long time.

Finally, in May 2013, following four years of college and one year since his father's diagnosis, Stephen and I had a come-to-Jesus conversation in my car at Sonic. It was a no-distractions place where we'd had several serious discussions before. This time, I desperately needed to know what kind of lifeline it would take to lift our son out of this enduring abyss. When would he finally be able to see a future for himself and move forward in a positive direction?

"Mom, I'm not ready to be the man of the house," he confessed through tears. "I just can't be the man you need me to be!"

I was stunned. Never had I asked him to step into that role. But now I understood that a tangle of complicated feelings was buried deep in all that mire, and he clearly needed more help than I could give.

The next day, I called a trusted psychologist. She listened closely as I shared information about Stephen's struggles and his father's disease.

"I work with a lot of college students," she assured me. "Coming to terms with the death of a parent is extremely difficult, and the student almost always loses a semester, a year, or more. Having a parent diagnosed with Alzheimer's is the next closest thing to having a parent die."

Our come-to-Jesus meeting and that phone call led to a breakthrough for our son as he began to identify and untangle his emotions. For years, Stephen had been assaulted by grief, blow after blow. The loss of his college sports dream, followed closely by the loss of his dad as he had known him, was overwhelming.

"Before that, nothing super bad had happened in my life," he later reflected. "It was so much at one time, and I didn't have the wherewithal to figure it all out. It seemed like my life was just falling apart. I was spiraling down and felt so lonely and depressed."

Like so many young people, when Stephen needed his family the most, he had pushed us away. Had we known what he was thinking, how he was feeling, perhaps we could have helped sooner.

"Looking back, it's hard to explain my mindset," he said. "If there is no Dad, what will Angela's life look like? What is this going to do to Mom? I never thought about myself, about dealing with my grief in a healthy way.

"That day in the car was a critical turning point. I finally realized, 'I just cannot do this anymore!'"

With God's healing, professional guidance, loving arms, and a newfound inner strength, Stephen worked his way through the grieving process to rediscover himself. TCU Graduation Day

2014 was one of our family's happiest celebrations. All dressed in Horned Frog purple, we were immensely proud to see Stephen moving forward with hope and confidence at last. His father cheered the loudest.

That summer, as their roles reversed, Stephen mapped the route and drove his dad across Texas on a tour of old army forts, fulfilling one of Steve's long-held desires.

Our ship may have been battered by the storm, but we had ridden the waves and had arrived safely at our next port. Surely, Jesus was in our boat.

CHAPTER 12

Brace Yourself

Above all, love each other deeply,
because love covers over a multitude of sins.

1 PETER 4:8 NIV

Cars on the roller coaster of life can range from the comfortable and secure to the cramped and rickety to everything in between. When riding in the Alzheimer's car, the turns are sharper, the slopes are steeper, and the loop-the-loops come when you least expect them. You have to brace yourself . . . a lot.

Experts say the onset of dementia occurs many years before the diagnosis. Observing his behaviors, I know this was true with Steve. I remember when he worked himself into a frenzy simply over a missing cell phone charger. Another evening, he angrily hurled an object across the room with little regard for what or who might be in the way . . . It hit me in the head. Shortly before his diagnosis, when he was again berating me for something or other one day, I snapped,

"You are *not* going to do to me what your father did to your mother!" That was not my proudest moment. Of course, I was referring to my father-in-law's bizarre behaviors, which were brought on by Alzheimer's and literally stressed my mother-in-law to death. I did not grasp then what I understand now about this cruel disease. And I was unaware Steve had it. All I was certain of was that these were not the behaviors of the man I married nor of the man our family, friends, and colleagues knew him to be.

Did I make my share of mistakes? Without a doubt . . . and more than my share. As they say, "You don't know what you don't know." What I didn't know about Alzheimer's disease at the beginning could fill a book and certainly has filled many. I've read some of them, trying to become a better caregiver. And I did learn over time. Still, challenges often presented themselves precisely when I forgot to use what I knew. Plus, there were occasions when Steve did not respond in textbook fashion. Only the Lord's guiding hand kept us from getting off-track and derailing completely.

Along the way, I met many *Aha!* moments, those welcome times of revelation and clarity. With them came plenty of *Huh?*, *Uh-oh!*, and *Oh no!* moments, plus the blessing of a few times that can only be described with a good-humored *Ha-ha!*

Early one morning in June 2014, Steve and I planned to drive south to Pearland, a suburb of Houston, to visit his brother and family, as well as to meet with our financial advisor.

As usual, little went as planned. After wrangling with a flat tire, misplaced car keys, and an uncooperative home security system, we were off at last.

Five minutes from home, Steve anxiously announced, "I don't

have my glasses! They were right here!" He pointed to the sunglass case lying on the console.

"I don't know where your sunglasses are," I replied. "Could they be in your pocket?"

"No. What did you do with them?"

"I didn't do anything. I don't have your sunglasses," I affirmed, wondering why he always accused me as if everything were my fault.

"Well, I guess they're gone!" he declared, clearly irritated, which could make for a long, uncomfortable drive for us both.

About five more minutes down the road, as we were stopped at a red light, I took off the sunglasses I was wearing. Then I saw clearly! The pair in my hand was tortoiseshell, like my own, but a different shape and brand.

Sheepishly, I reached into my purse and pulled out my own sunglasses, which had been hiding there all along.

Handing Steve the pair I had been wearing, I profusely apologized. This time it really was my fault.

"I am so sorry! These are *your* sunglasses. I must have picked them up off the console, thinking they were mine. I had no idea I had them on this whole time. Please forgive me!"

I nervously braced myself for the explosion that was sure to come . . . Instead, Steve burst into laughter. "Great!" he said, putting them on with a smile.

It was a God-given *Ha-ha!* moment.

Turns out I had on mismatched earrings that day too.

The *Huh?* moments were generally a guessing game of verbal charades as Steve increasingly lost his ability to find the right words—specifically, nouns.

About ten minutes from home, on our return trip from Pearland, we stopped at a favorite café and picked up two boxed lunches to go.

As we continued our drive, Steve asked, "How do we open the boxes?"

"Do you mean our lunch?" I asked.

"How do we get to the boxes? The boxes for Friday and Saturday." He was becoming restless.

Finally, it dawned on me. We were approaching home, where his world now revolved around his television. The "boxes" were the rectangles of the television guide timetable in the newspaper, where he obsessively spent hours underlining and circling all the shows he wanted to see. He was anxious about what he could watch over the weekend.

A month later, our travel agent friend was meeting with me in our kitchen to finalize our Hawaiian vacation plans.

Steve interrupted us, asking impatiently, "So how do I manage?"

We were puzzled. Manage what, exactly?

"The schedule," he said. "It's in a box."

Aha! This time I understood. "Oh, you're talking about the TV! We can work that out," I tried to reassure him.

But like so many things, that "we" became "I" when he no longer could comprehend when his favorite shows aired, how to record them, or how to find and play back what had been recorded.

Fortunately, we got a little break from all that in Maui.

Unfortunately, in addition to those involving verbal charades, there were countless other *Huh?* moments to come. Steve desperately wanted an extremely expensive analog watch, when he could no longer tell time. He wanted the newest, best-selling novel, when he had lost most of his ability to read. And, of course, he wanted the most updated television device available, when he could no longer learn how to use it.

Just the thought of a routine colonoscopy is a kind of *Uh-oh!* moment for anyone. Add Alzheimer's into the picture, and there is nothing "routine" about it.

Prior to Steve's scheduled procedure, I had completed his paperwork, adding a note that he had Alzheimer's disease. On the morning of his colonoscopy, I drove him to the day surgery center and accompanied him to the check-in desk when his name was called.

A printed sign posted above the desk read, "Please state your name and date of birth."

After greeting us both, the woman behind the desk instructed Steve, "Read the sign and do what it says."

He became the deer in the headlights.

"Read the sign and do what it says," she repeated sternly.

I was becoming annoyed. She had his paperwork in her hand. Had no one read it? If they failed to see that he had Alzheimer's, had they failed to review his other medical history as well? Although I always tried to refrain from talking about Steve in front of him, this time I had no choice.

"He has Alzheimer's disease," I whispered to her.

"But he still needs to read the sign," she replied indignantly.

This was unbelievable. "He can't!" I exclaimed, my voice getting louder. Why couldn't she understand? "He has Alzheimer's disease," I repeated. "It's on his paperwork. The whole point of putting it there was to avoid something like this. I am his wife, and I can read the sign!"

Then I may have shouted his name and birth date at her— without apology.

But that was only the beginning ...

More than an hour had passed since Steve had been escorted into the patient area when the nurse anxiously came into the waiting room looking for me.

"I need you to come back with me," she said.

When I did, I saw Steve dressed in a hospital gown, sitting up in a bed, with an IV in his arm and rivers of agitation coursing through his veins. The procedure had not even started. Unfortunately, the doctor who was to perform his colonoscopy had been detained by a medical emergency at the hospital. It had been an exceedingly long wait, and Steve was getting more and more fretful by the minute. I sat in the chair beside him in an effort to calm him down. Trying to think of a distraction, I asked the nurse if someone could find a newspaper and a pen so he could circle his beloved television shows for a while.

"Get this thing out of me!" he yelled, tugging on his IV line.

"I'm sorry, I can't do that," I said. "I know it's been a long wait and you are tired of this. I don't blame you. The doctor will be here soon."

"Then I'll pull it out myself!"

I jumped to my feet. "Oh, that's not a good idea!"

"Take me home!" he shouted.

"I can't," I responded.

"Then I'll drive myself!"

"You can't."

"Then I will divorce you!"

Clearly, I was not handling this well. His refusal to calm down and stay put only became more vehement.

That day, the four best words in the English language were, "The doctor is in." And on that day, I vowed that Steve would never have another colonoscopy as long as we both shall live.

As the name suggests, *Oh no!* moments were the most troublesome.

On a crisp, cold February afternoon, Steve and I met Angela and a friend of hers at a restaurant for a late, leisurely (or so I hoped) Saturday brunch. We had not had a good, long visit with our daughter since Christmas, and although her friend was temporarily living in our guesthouse, we seldom got the chance to chat with her.

Our server was refilling our glasses when Steve started looking nervously at the watch he habitually wore. I was certain he could no longer read it correctly. On numerous occasions, I had asked him if he would like a digital watch, and always his answer was an emphatic "No!"

"Honey, is there somewhere you need to be?" I asked when his foot began tapping impatiently.

With a roll of his eyes, he answered, "I have to go."

"Where do you have to be?"

"Four o'clock," he responded.

"What happens at four?" I wanted to know.

Repeatedly, he poked at his watch and replied in exasperation, "Four o'clock. Soccer. Soccer comes on at four."

"Well, Steve, it's only two thirty. We have plenty of time to be home by four." I reminded him that our house was only ten minutes away. "Can't we just enjoy each other a little while longer?"

"I'm leaving now!" he announced.

"We don't even have the bill yet, and the car is valet parked. How are you going to get home?" I asked in a foolish attempt to reason with him.

"I'll walk!" he said as he stood, put on his coat, and rushed out the door.

I quickly paid the bill and called for my car. As I drove up and down the surrounding streets looking for Steve, I called 911 from my cell phone. The police dispatcher on the line advised me to go home and see if he showed up there.

Meanwhile, Angela in her own car followed the route she assumed he would take and, thankfully, found him three blocks from our house.

"Get in the car, Dad," she said, and he did.

From that day forward, whenever Steve wanted to leave, we left. As much as possible, I determined to do what he wanted to do when he wanted to do it. I may have been the caregiver and decision-maker, but the disease was now in charge. Time to brace ourselves for an even wilder ride.

CHAPTER 13

Playing His Part

So in everything,
do to others what you would have them do to you,
for this sums up the Law and the Prophets.

MATTHEW 7:12 NIV

What is it like to live with a person who has Alzheimer's? Simply put, it is hard. It can be discouraging and exhausting. It can be exasperating, overwhelming, and excruciatingly lonely. Sometimes, it feels as though you are repeatedly hitting your head against an impenetrable stone wall until, without warning, it shatters like glass. At other times, it feels as if you are balancing on a teetering tightrope over a safety net with a gaping hole just daring you to fall through.

But what is it like to actually have the disease? That I don't know. Aside from reading the research and trusting the experts,

I can only speculate, imagine, and, on occasion, vividly dream, as recorded in my journal:

> I dreamed I was in a dress rehearsal for a play. When we got to the second act, I not only couldn't remember my lines, but I was entirely confused as to where we were in the plot. I kept asking for help. When someone handed me a script, I looked and looked through all the pages but could not find my place. Fellow actors guided me on and off the stage and tried to remind me what was happening next. I would say, "Oh, yes!" although I really didn't remember. I was completely lost. All I could do was apologize. "I am the person who has always had her lines perfectly memorized," I said. "I am so sorry. I don't know what happened!"

For some, this scenario may not seem too frightening, but for anyone who has ever performed onstage, it is a nightmare. I woke up in a sweat, wondering if that is how it feels to have Alzheimer's.

To move beyond dreams, speculation, and imagination, I took advantage of an extraordinary program wherein participants with healthy brains virtually experience what it is like to have dementia.

Before entering the designated, unoccupied room at a local residential memory care facility, the other program participant and I had some preparation to do. First, we were outfitted with goggles that greatly restricted our vision. This was to simulate the effects that dementia has on sight, such as decreased peripheral vision, as well as the effects of cataracts, glaucoma, or macular degeneration that many older individuals have. Next, we put on large, ill-fitting gloves that limited our dexterity and fine motor skills. Then, uncomfortable, spiky pads were placed in our shoes to imitate neuropathy. Lastly, we were given earphones that played an incessant babble of noise in the background to confuse our brains.

The facilitator spoke a set of five tasks to my partner and then a different set of five tasks to me. All could be accomplished in this one room. We had only a few minutes to complete them. Ready, set, go!

Immediately, I had a problem. Through all the clamor coming from the earphones, I only clearly heard three of the tasks. Still, thinking those should not be too difficult, I embarked on the first: "Find the belt and put it on."

I looked in the closet, but with my goggles on, it was too dark to see much of anything there. I opened drawers, which was not easy in those clumsy gloves. My partner was talking to himself as he entered the bathroom on a finding mission of his own. Maybe he had a good idea! Although that was not a usual place for a belt, it could be hiding in the shower. I followed him in and followed him out. After looking over both beds and under all the pillows, I sat down and started laughing out loud. This was ridiculous! I could not see, my feet hurt, and the constant chatter in my head was incredibly annoying and distracting.

Nevertheless, I persevered. Determined to find the belt, I searched the back side of an open door and beheld my prize at last. "Hooray!" I shouted. I managed to take the belt off the hook and place it around my waist, but buckling it was another matter altogether. Those awful gloves! Fumbling to get the belt through just one loop, I left the end flapping around so I could proceed to the next task: "Find the notepad and pen and write a note." I had barely begun my new hunt when the time was up.

What a revelational experience that was! I now understood

why dementia patients wandered the rooms in their homes and the hallways in care facilities—they were looking for something. Out of sheer frustration with our limited abilities to perform the tasks, my partner continually murmured to himself, and I giggled and heaved deep sighs at the most unexpected times. Now I could appreciate why patients mutter and have all kinds of verbal outbursts. Surprising even myself, I had called out, "Hooray!" when no one else knew what I was celebrating. If the exercise had lasted much longer, I am certain at least one of us would have started cursing. And because I physically could not fully buckle the belt, I just gave up and moved on to something else. I didn't care. No wonder patients wear mismatched clothing with buttons askew and zippers awry.

How I wish I had experienced this program earlier in Steve's journey with this disease! It gave me a new level of empathy, not only for him but also for every person with dementia. I began to realize that the frustration I was feeling when trying to figure out what Steve was saying paled in comparison to the frustration he must feel all day every day. Being unable to communicate with or understand others is terrifying. And everything else that comes with Alzheimer's must be at least equally frightening.

Life, regrettably, has no dress rehearsal like in my dream. Every dawn brings an opening night performance. I envision the best I can what it must be like to play Steve's part. I only wish we had a different script.

CHAPTER 14

Heaven Can't Wait

Blessed are those who mourn,
for they shall be comforted.

MATTHEW 5:4 RSV

From the outset, I determined not to tell my parents about Steve's diagnosis. I loved them too much. My father, whom I had seen cry only twice in my life, would surely make it a third after hearing the news. My mother, who was battling vascular dementia, would pretend to understand and sweetly inquire, "What can I do for *you?*" It was a question she asked on each of my daily visits. At that point, she could do very little for herself, much less for anyone else. Still, it came from a special place in her heart.

When Mom broke her hip just after Thanksgiving 2007, Steve was commuting to Dallas, Angela was a freshman at TCU, and Stephen was a high school junior. Although I already was accompanying my parents on their frequent doctors' visits, the scheduling, driving, and medication management immediately became my sole responsibility. I did their weekly grocery shopping and visited CVS so frequently that the pharmacists and I greeted one another on a first-name basis. Because my mom was no longer able to set and style her own hair as she always had, I routinely took her to a beauty salon that catered to many of her friends. To aid in my parents' comfort, I arranged for a massage therapist to come to the house occasionally and for a sweet and patient nail technician to give them manicures and pedicures at home. In a final effort to save the last glimmer of Daddy's eyesight, Jody and I drove him to numerous surgeries in Dallas. Jody handled their finances while I oversaw the paid caregiver duties. Eventually, we had wheelchair ramps installed for Mom and grab bars strategically placed throughout the house for Dad.

As my parents declined physically, transporting them to and from their doctors' offices became next to impossible for me. What a blessing that we were able to get them both on hospice, with a nurse coming to check on them every week. That did a lot for our peace of mind. Still, meeting their increasing needs in a loving, devoted manner was all-consuming.

"If I had a full-time job," I confided in Angie back then, while she lived in Virginia, "I would have to quit."

Not that I was resentful. I wasn't. But I was tired, and it was mentally and emotionally difficult for me to pull myself away from their world and back into the one that existed for my husband and children. As I was racing out the door to my parents' house one afternoon, I told Stephen that I hoped I was modeling biblical and loving behavior for him.

"Oh, Mom, I'm just going to put you in a home," he said offhandedly.

"Well, please save your money and make sure it's a good one!" I responded with a laugh as I pondered how serious he might or might not be.

Angie's return to Fort Worth in the summer of 2012 was a tremendous boost to our family in every way. Not only did her presence lift my spirits, but she also quickly jumped in to share responsibilities and take multiple duties off my shoulders. In addition to helping with the daily and weekly chores, she assumed others as well. One of those was changing out the flowers at the gravesite where previous generations of our family were buried. Back in the 1960s, our parents and grandparents had selected a stone monument with two vases in the design. For decades, our mother had filled those vases each season with carefully arranged artificial flowers. After she broke her hip, it became my job, until my sister stepped in. As in most things, Angie was more consistent and creative in her approach than I ever was.

By late 2014, the caregiving team in our parents' home was thoroughly overwhelmed. Mom forgot she could no longer walk and fell out of her wheelchair, breaking her femur and requiring more surgery on her frail body. Having survived a heart attack, melanoma, sepsis, and loss of his optic nerve, Dad was now totally blind. Additionally, late-onset Parkinson's disease was taking its toll on him mentally and physically. Meeting their mounting needs was more than any one caregiver could handle.

Angie, Jody, and I came together for an agonizing family meeting. Our parents had been adamant that they never wanted to move out of our family home. How could we respect their wishes while meeting their needs? We felt we had no choice.

After touring two well-respected long-term care facilities, both located nearby, we chose to move them to the James L. West Center for Dementia Care. Although they would reside in different areas, the staff promised to take our father to visit our mother regularly. Because of Dad's blindness and increasing withdrawal, he was placed in a wing with residents needing the most care. Mom would live on a different floor, where several of her friends with dementia already resided. Their moving day was one of the saddest of my life, and the guilt that moved into my heart that day still remains. As much as I never wanted to see Daddy cry again, he met me tear for tear.

Either my siblings or I visited our parents every day. And day by day, we watched in sorrow as our beloved father slipped away from us. One afternoon, thinking he was sitting in his old comfy recliner, Dad pushed back in his wheelchair and fell to the floor, hitting his head hard. For years, he had responded to my saying "I love you!" by echoing it back or replying, "Thank you, darlin'." Now there was silence. This is not how my brave and beloved father would want to live. Each time I left him, I prayed the Lord would take him to his heavenly home . . . My prayers were soon answered. Exactly one month after the move, Daddy died in his sleep.

We decided not to tell our mother. She was flourishing in her own way at the West Center. Instead of sitting in the bedroom watching television with my dad, as she had done during the days at home, she became her unit's unofficial hostess, attempting to make sure everyone was happy. She watched her longtime friend do wheelchair laps up and down the hall, and she learned to do the same. Group activities like music therapy and art made her smile.

All things considered, we were amazed Mom was doing so well. She was, as she would say, "a people person," and now she was enjoying nurturing others in her own way, as well as being nurtured herself. Soon after a lifelong friend of mine moved her mother into the same unit, she shared with me this lasting impression:

When we brought Mother up, it was in the evening before dinner. Your mother saw mine coming in on her walker. She reached out with a gesture with both hands extended to welcome her. It was as if she was in her own home extending her gracious spirit. Seeing your mother, fair-haired with the sweetest smile and twinkle in her eyes, was like being greeted by an angel. We had prayed fervently about this decision to place our dear mother in a dementia care facility. It was like the Lord welcomed Mother and us by using your mom. I will never forget the feeling that it was the right time and that God had not forgotten Mother nor all the precious friends on that floor.

Sadly, not everyone appreciated Mom's attentiveness quite as much. As I sat beside her in the hallway one day, a lady rolled past us in her wheelchair as quickly as her frail arms could push. For several days, my mother had fixated on this particular resident, fussing over her in every detail. By now, it was evident to me that the woman was no longer enjoying the uninvited attention, as she took every opportunity to distance herself from us. We watched her stop in the dining area and start picking at her clothes.

"Oh that poor thing! She needs me. I have to go help her," Mom said with compassion.

"I think she's okay, Mom. I really do. Let's just stay here," I responded with compassion from a differing viewpoint.

"That's *not* how we do things!" she scolded me as she wheeled away to tend to her "guest."

Our parent-child roles had reversed—she didn't remember she was my mother, and yet, somehow, she was still compelled to teach me manners. All I could do was laugh.

One afternoon, Angie and I visited Mom and found her just inside the doorway, encircled by her doctor and a group of medical students. Naturally, we were concerned.

"We were just giving your mother some cognitive tests," the doctor reassured us. "I asked her to write a sentence. Would you like to see what she wrote?"

My sister and I looked at each other in astonishment. Mom could write a sentence? It had been years since she had been able to write a note, a sentence, or even a word on her prized pink stationery. Of course we wanted to see! Her handwriting was slanted, but the words and message were clear: "I love my family." What a blessed reminder that the amazing mother who raised us was still in there . . . somewhere.

Our devoted parents had been married almost seventy-two years when Daddy died. We always believed they would pass within a few weeks, if not days, of each other. As it happened, it was almost three months. In late February 2015, I got the call.

"There has been a significant change in your mother," the nurse said. "Her vital signs are not good. I would get the family here as quickly as possible."

Angie, Jody, and I went immediately to find Mom lying in her bed and receiving oxygen. We called our spouses and children, and I asked if one of them would please drive Steve over. Several of her grandchildren were able to come and say goodbye to their beloved "Mimi." She lovingly told Angela that she was beautiful, and that she was proud of her.

Together, my sister and I went into Mom's room. Her eyes were open, but the oxygen tank was loud, and she spoke in a whisper.

"Joe told me," she said. Joe was our father.

"What did Joe tell you?" I asked.

Her answer was faint, and we strained in vain to hear it. But we were certain Joe was telling her it was time to join him in the heavenly arms of Jesus.

Looking at Angie and me, she added, "Take care of yourselves. I'll miss you."

That afternoon, she closed her eyes and spoke no more. A few days later, she was reunited with her precious Joe. Theirs was a true love story.

Following the visitation for my mother at the funeral home, our family gathered at Angie and Butch's house to comfort one another over dinner. Yes, there was a large, creamy casserole, provided by a friend. In the kitchen, Angela's longtime boyfriend, Matt, gently pulled me aside.

"Kathe, I know this probably isn't the best time to bring this up, but I would like to come talk to you and Steve sometime very soon. If possible, I'd like for Stephen to be there, too," he said.

"Actually, Matt, this is a fine time," I replied. I knew he wanted to receive our blessing before proposing to our daughter, and, Lord knows, we all needed a happy, new focus. "When would you like to come?"

CHAPTER 15

For Better, For Worse

Likewise the Spirit helps us in our weakness;
for we do not know how to pray as we ought,
but the Spirit himself intercedes for us
with sighs too deep for words.

ROMANS 8:26 RSV

Few questions are more life-changing than "Will you marry me?" Matt proposed; Angela accepted. Undoubtedly, she realized the significance of her upcoming vows. Throughout her life, she had seen her father and me love and cherish each other during the good times and the not-so-good. She had observed our commitment both in sickness and in health. She had experienced the better and lately witnessed too much of the worse. And she knew we were dedicated not only to have, but also to hold on . . .

We had a wedding to plan! Who better to assist us than my sister? Angie was the consummate, detail-oriented, no-time-to-lose administrator. Day to day, moment by moment, I tried to remember to ask myself, "What would Jesus do?" Before undertaking any big project, I also pondered, "What would Angie do?" She would get organized! Thus, out came a hefty, new three-ring binder with multiple dividers that came to be known as the Wedding Notebook. It grew fatter by the week.

Angela and Matt had their hearts set on a spring 2016 outdoor ceremony. Any thought of a destination wedding—even one within a few hours' driving distance—was dismissed because of Steve's increasing needs and decreasing ability to be left alone for lengthy periods of time. It just would have been too difficult, if not impossible, to plan. After weeks of research, they agreed on an April 16 wedding in the Fort Worth Botanic Garden, followed by a reception at the country club.

While we were off and running toward Angela's dream wedding, however, her dad's nightmarish disease was crippling his mind even further. We entered a race against the clock, with hurdles looming around every turn.

I had no concept of how bad Steve's "worse" might truly get. While he could still perform routine chores—bringing in the newspaper, feeding our dog, Nora, taking the trash and recycling bins to and from the curb—the changes in his brain were manifesting themselves in distressing ways. He seemed to require me and resent me in equal measure.

"We have a problem!" is how he began to greet me in the morning and each time I entered a room. More often than not, the problem involved what was showing—or not showing—on TV. I wish I had known how to use a streaming service back then! When I tried to explain to him that it was impossible to watch the movie *Top Gun* at two o'clock in the afternoon because we hadn't recorded it when it had aired at eight o'clock that morning, he exclaimed, "You're not helping me!" I was trying the best I knew how. But there is no point in attempting to reason with a person who has lost the ability to understand.

Televised soccer, played by any team, anywhere, anytime, had become one of Steve's obsessions. For several months, our nephew, J.D., came to watch it with Steve at least once a week. He would sit patiently with his uncle for hours, commenting on the game and keeping him good company. When I repeatedly thanked J.D., he always replied, "It's just soccer." But to Steve and to me, it was so much more.

As long as I continued the daily routine of taking Steve out for lunch, I was still able to leave him in front of the TV for a few hours while I ran errands, met friends, or went to appointments. My visit to the hair salon was long overdue, and I was happily sitting in front of my stylist with my hair wrapped in pieces of foil when my cell phone rang. It was our housekeeper, who came twice a month and whom I had left at home with Steve that morning.

"I can't! I can't! Your husband!" Speaking with limited English, she sounded panicked and breathless.

"Are you okay? Get out of the house!" I responded without hesitation. If not for the bleach and strips of metal in my hair, I would have kept her on the line while I exceeded every speed limit to get home.

"I am. I did. I'm scared!" Of course she was frightened. Steve had screamed at her and become aggressive when she attempted to clean the den, putting all ninety pounds of herself between him and his all-important television.

"I am so very sorry," I said, knowing exactly how she felt. "I promise I will never leave you alone with Steve again."

Unfortunately, I didn't get the opportunity to make good on my promise—she refused to come back. Once again, I felt as if a vacuum cleaner had sucked me up, thrashed me about, and spat me back out.

Regrettably, I could think of little else besides TV to keep Steve occupied. Even in his most vibrant years, he had such high expectations of himself that if he could not do something well, he chose not to do it at all. Early in our married life, he had enjoyed playing golf until the demands of his job kept him off the course. Reading, playing cards, and working puzzles—from crossword to jigsaw—had ranked among his favorite pastimes at home. Now, not only could he not do them well, but they had also become impossible for him. My suggestions of activities not involving TV were met with an indignant, "I want to do what *I want to do!*" In the support group, I heard that people with dementia typically enjoy folding things, like linens and towels. During all our years of marriage, the only thing I had ever seen Steve fold was a stack of meticulously selected shirts to pack in a travel bag. As he sat in his leather chair with the TV remote in one hand and the dog curled up at his feet, I couldn't imagine that he would willingly start folding now.

His sense of time became more and more confused. One early morning, he awakened at three o'clock and went through his entire shower, shave, contact lenses, get-dressed-for-the-day routine. Another day, he changed clothes at eleven in the morning for an outing with a friend that was scheduled at four o'clock that afternoon.

That friend never knew how esteemed he was, as changing clothes had become a rarity for Steve. My husband, who once had exquisite taste in clothing, now was content to wear the same shirt and pair of shorts for a week. He would have worn the same pajamas and underwear too, had I not stealthily picked them up off the floor and washed them.

If I asked him to dress in a pair of khaki slacks for dinner out, he yelled at me. Yet when a dear friend's father died, Steve willingly donned a suit for the memorial service. Standing outside his bathroom door, I could hear him heaving deeply labored sighs. I knocked to enter and found him staring into the mirror and sweating profusely with a tie loosely draped around his neck. This sixty-four-year-old man who had worn a necktie every single day of his working life had forgotten how to tie one. Thank goodness we live in the internet age. I searched "how to tie a tie" and followed the YouTube video. Steve tightened the knot with a smile. Crisis averted.

At least he didn't have as many suits and ties to choose from as he'd once had. After departing the law firm, he certainly didn't need them all. Just as I had known that I couldn't be the one to tell him he could no longer drive, I recognized that someone else needed to direct the necessary closet purge. The logical person to do this was the same sales representative who had enticed Steve to buy all that custom-tailored apparel in the first place. He agreed to come for a fee.

"Steve, I think you still have the first suit I ever sold you way back in the eighties," he said when he entered the closet. Like me, he could almost hear the rods groaning under the weight of all those clothes. With his trusted fashion consultant's guidance, Steve was happy to banish whatever was deemed outworn, outdated, or unnecessary. And I was happy to donate it all to charity.

No matter what he was wearing, the moment Steve stopped going to work, he routinely expected that we would go out to lunch together every day. So, with few exceptions, we did. At first, I too looked forward to these daily outings. I enjoyed our conversations and sampling new restaurants. Plus a good, filling meal at noon meant we could get by with soup or cereal for dinner, which was fine with me because I didn't particularly enjoy cooking. Occasionally, we would run into friends or acquaintances on these lunch outings.

"Hey, Steve, why aren't you in the office?" one inquired after seeing him dressed so casually midweek.

"I retired! I got tired of driving to Dallas," he eagerly replied.

In a sense, that was true, and it was neither the time nor the place for me to offer further explanation.

Over the years, however, the lunch routine became more drudgery for me than delight. Steve wanted to visit the same restaurants over and over and order the same thing. (I understand now that it was part of his "comfort zone.") His ability to make pleasant conversation—almost any conversation—was severely altered. And his unpredictable behavior made me and sometimes those around us uneasy. After one memorable public incident, I took the experts' advice and began carrying pocket-sized cards that began with these words: "Please pardon my companion who has

Alzheimer's disease." I never knew when I might need to slip one to a confused server or disapproving onlooker.

When Angie, Butch, and Jody took him to TCU Frog Club luncheons during football season or when one of his loyal friends picked him up for an outing, I was immensely grateful for the break. But on each occasion, I held my breath and said a prayer that Steve's actions would not cause this to be the last such invitation.

At home, Steve began shadowing, following me from room to room. Perhaps he wondered if I knew something he didn't, just as I had wondered during the virtual dementia experience when I started following my partner. Still, his shadowing was not healthy for either of us. It accentuated my stress level as now, more than ever, I needed physical room to breathe.

If he could not find something he wanted, which happened frequently, he immediately accused me of stealing it. Painfully few discoveries resulted in the kind of laughter we shared over his lost-and-found sunglasses.

Never one to be suspicious in the past, Steve now became overly so. "What is this? Why is it yours?" he demanded to know when an unsolicited credit card offer, addressed to me, arrived in the mail. The fact that I had received countless such offers over the years, considered them junk mail, and threw them in the recycling bin did not matter.

Truthfully, I did secure one credit card solely in my name without telling him. He was beyond understanding the reasons why. Every card in my wallet had been linked to his primary account and Social Security number in one way or another. With an eye toward the future, I realized I needed to finally establish some credit on my own. Earning frequent flier miles or other points in *my* name along the way was an additional benefit.

While Steve always had been tidy, he also had been reluctant to throw anything away. This tendency was so compounded by his disease that he became somewhat of a hoarder. Although I had thankfully found assistance with the clothes, there was no one who could help with all the rest.

As consumed as Steve was with television, he had become equally obsessed with the newspaper. What began with daily circling of the TV programs he wanted to watch or record eventually developed into underscoring every single line of text. For Steve, only a particular kind of pen was suited for this task, so we stocked up every two weeks at the office supply store.

While the essence of a daily newspaper is to be read today and recycled tomorrow, that theory did not sit well with my husband. Beside his favorite chair, the pile of papers grew like the trees they originated from. Heaven forbid they should vanish entirely! I learned to remove a few from the bottom of the pile every now and then when he was not looking.

All of those troublesome tendencies, however, paled in comparison to Steve's mounting combativeness. What often began as frustration led to agitation that escalated into anger and exploded in aggression. His boiling point had lowered, and he was already simmering much of the time. I loved my husband, but I hated and feared this disease. I tried to help, to intervene, to redirect the best I knew how.

Our children perceived the change. Angela was especially aware of it, as we were spending numerous hours together working on wedding details. Jody, Patti, and Butch observed it firsthand. And my devoted sister was on high alert. Except for a very few in whom I confided, our friends were completely unaware of this grim aspect of Steve's disease. In one sense, I wanted to protect his reputation. In another, I didn't want to burden our friends because there was nothing they could do.

With increasing regularity, I sought safety behind my locked bathroom door as my dear husband lashed out at me verbally and physically. He shouted. Loudly. He slammed doors with such force that the entire house seemed to shake. On occasion, he would throw whatever was handy at the wall or at me. More than once, I emerged from the bathroom to find our dog, Nora, on the other side of the door, silently pleading to be let in. She was fearful too. When each episode was over, Steve behaved as though nothing had happened. He had forgotten entirely.

Try as I might not to let my own emotions get the best of me, I often wept in my bathtub at midnight. Sometimes I curled up in the fetal position on our bed at midday. During an earlier, excruciatingly low point in my life, I penned this chorus to a song with no verses:

> It's like bleeding out on the inside,
> It's like going to hell on a carpet ride,
> It's like death before suicide.
> But somehow, I'll get by.
> With God's help, I'll get by.

Now those words kept looping in my head as complete verses were being played out on our very worst days.

On a mid-March afternoon, Angela and I were sitting at the kitchen table attempting to finalize a few wedding details. Each time we initiated a discussion, her dad walked in from the TV room and anxiously exclaimed, "We have a problem!" or angrily accused, "You're not helping me!" This happened over and over even though I repeatedly got up from the table and tried to address the issue.

Finally, Angela asked with notable concern, "Mom, *what* are you going to do?" I knew the question was not about that particular day but rather about the ones to come.

"Hold on until your wedding on April sixteenth," I replied with my fingers crossed and a prayer in my heart.

Sadly, it was not to be. The disease was conducting the orchestra, and by the following weekend, it had reached a crescendo. Steve's forceful outbursts escalated in intensity and frequency.

I phoned the Alzheimer's Association Helpline and left my number. When someone returned my call, I was attending to Steve's needs and unable to answer. I tried calling Angie. She always picked up when I called, but not this time. She and Butch were at a Saturday afternoon TCU baseball game, and she did not hear her phone. When we talked later that evening, she expressed her growing worries about me and offered her home as a retreat. I gratefully declined as I felt it unwise to leave Steve alone.

The next day was Palm Sunday. Just when I thought we had reached a peaceful interlude following church and lunch, the cymbals clashed again. At my request, Jody came over and attempted to calm his brother-in-law and old friend.

While my brother distracted my husband, I pondered what the coming evening, the next few days, and the four weeks leading up to Angela and Matt's wedding would look like. Steve had repeatedly and angrily threatened to harm himself. Was it just a matter of time before he threatened to harm me too? Although I knew it was the Alzheimer's talking, I also knew there was a chance it could cause him to act on those threats. If he did, how could I stop him? He was bigger, faster, and stronger. More than anything, I did not want our children to lose both of their parents anytime soon.

At some point in my Alzheimer's research, I had read that if an individual feels she is in imminent danger from someone with dementia, she should call 911, ask to speak with a mental health officer, and inform that person of the disease. That way, the first responders will take the aggressor to a hospital rather than to jail. I stored the information away somewhere in my brain, hoping against hope that I never would have to use it.

But that unforgettable Sunday would see those hopes shattered. Shortly after Jody left, the dysfunctional orchestra in Steve's mind banged the bass drum to a thunderous, threatening roar. He was standing between me and the stairs leading to my safe place. My heart was pounding. I grabbed my cell phone and walked out the back door and through the gate to the street as fast as I could. Steve followed. As he still easily could outwalk me, I picked up my pace and made the call I had hoped I never would.

By the time the paramedics arrived, I had reached the corner of our street, and Steve was right behind me. He was perfectly calm, even smiling, as he told me he thought we were walking to Target to buy him a new DVD—something we had never done before. When the police arrived, they saw him fully cooperating with the emergency medical technicians, who were taking his vital signs.

For a moment, I considered reversing course, telling them all "never mind" and walking Steve back home . . . But then what? Would I be calling 911 again tonight? Tomorrow? What if my next instinct to call came too late? With the Alzheimer's thief sneaking around in there, our home had ceased to be a safe place for either one of us.

I watched in agony as the ambulance drove away with the man I had vowed "to love and to cherish" thirty-seven years before. The symphony had left the hall.

CHAPTER 16

Our Newer Reality

Let the morning bring me word of your unfailing love,
for I have put my trust in you.
Show me the way I should go, for to you I entrust my life.

PSALM 143:8 NIV

More often than not, when it seems your world changes in an instant, it is actually a series of changes that have led to that moment. That was certainly true in our case.

Following a surreal, sleepless night reflecting on the 911 call and all that led up to it, I arranged a family meeting. Stephen, Angie and Butch, and Jody and Patti were there. Angela and Matt brought a fajita dinner for the group, reminding me that all news, whether good or bad, goes down better with food. While everyone knew bits and pieces of what had transpired over the weekend, I prayed we would be unified in our mission to achieve what was best for Steve and for our family. Truthfully, I was unsure how each of them would react.

A mix of emotions came out. Sadness and support. Sympathy and understanding. Relief is the reaction that surprised me the most. Memorably, Angela expressed it best.

"My first concern has been your safety, Mom," she confided.

Exhaling a deep breath, she continued, "And, honestly, I have been so worried about how Dad might be on the night of our wedding." Even though we had alternate plans and extra assistance in place, she was anxious it would not be enough. "What if he decided not to walk me all the way down the aisle? What would we do if he had an outburst? What if he got restless and wanted to leave the reception early?"

Bless her beautiful heart! Along with the usual stress of being a bride, she had been carrying all that additional apprehension. As we talked around the table, I reflected on what Matt had sweetly told Angela a year before their engagement: "I will marry you tomorrow if you're worried that your dad might not be able to walk you down the aisle." He had long been saving for an engagement ring, and our crystal ball was murky at best.

While each family member raged silently against the disease that had led us all to this moment, no one expressed anger at me or even questioned my actions. Indeed, they had realized for years, as I had, that although Steve would never willingly move to a long-term memory facility, he would eventually require that level of care. We just had not known when would be the right time or where would be the right place.

This was the time; now we had to find the place.

What I did not realize when I called 911 was that I would have no say in what happened to Steve over the next several days.

Within twenty-four hours, he was transferred from an acute care hospital to one specializing in psychiatric care, which had extremely restrictive policies on everything, including visitation. Nevertheless, I needed to see Steve. He needed clean clothes and his contact lenses. And Angie, in her big-sisterly way, needed to go with me.

What a shock to my system! The meeting area was cold and austere. Observing the handful of psychiatric patients who were fortunate enough to have visitors was yet another stinging reminder that "everybody has their stuff," much of which is heartbreaking. Steve was understandably confused, but non-confrontational, and glad to see us. Then almost as soon as our visit began, we were told it was time to leave.

During Steve's stay, I went to see him every day—sometimes alone, other times with a sibling or one of our children.

Angela visited within the first few days. "I was so worried about Dad being alone and afraid and confused. I didn't want him to feel defeated and small. Of course, he wanted to go home, but he didn't have that choice. It all made me feel so helpless. I don't even know how to describe it," she later told me.

Stephen's visit came several days later. When Steve saw him, he cheered, "Finally!" and greeted him with a fatherly hug.

Upon Steve's arrival, the doctor at the psychiatric hospital immediately started him on antidepressants, antipsychotics, and anti-anxiety medications—something I had been reluctant to do at home. My prior research cautioned that some of these medications could have serious, even fatal side effects and that using them to manage behavior in dementia patients should only be a last resort. In hindsight, they might have been worth the risk. Then maybe

Steve could have stayed home longer. But now he was in the hands of medical experts . . . or so I thought.

In reciting the list of Steve's symptoms, behaviors, and diagnoses to me, the staff doctor included bipolar disorder.

"Steve has Alzheimer's disease," I corrected him. "He is not now, nor has he ever been, bipolar. Please take that off his records."

"Don't worry about it," he countered. "No one is going to look at that. It won't matter in the future."

He was wrong. I should have fought him harder.

In the meantime, I needed to find the best possible placement for my dear husband. The sooner the better. Angie and I searched the internet separately and together. We narrowed down the list and began visiting each one. Immediately, we were dismayed and disheartened by what we found.

Standing in a steamy parking lot on a late Friday afternoon after yet another disappointing and depressing tour, the Lord reminded my spirit of the words a sweet friend had spoken to me months earlier: "When the time is right, Kathe, you should consider the new memory care community where my father lives." Instantly, I recalled the facility's name.

"Shall we call right now?" I asked Angie.

"Absolutely!" she encouraged. We jumped into my car and cranked up the AC.

A gracious staff member agreed to give us a five o'clock tour that very day. As Angie and I exited the tollway and saw the building, I had a brief *Aha!* moment. I knew this place! For the past year, I had been singing with a group of Junior League sustaining members called the Sunshine Singers. We were a chorus of old and new friends whose mission was to bring showtunes with smiles to senior living and memory care communities. When we had entertained here just a few months before, it never occurred to me that I would be back so soon in an entirely new role.

Our tour guide was unhurried as she showed us the large, open courtyard, the welcoming dining area, the bistro stations scattered throughout, and the friendly dogs and cats who called this place home. Unlike some other buildings, where residents with dementia were confined to a specific floor or wing, the entire facility and all the staff were devoted to memory care. We liked what we saw, but we were at the end of yet another extremely long and trying day.

The next morning, while the coffee was brewing, I came within a few short breaths of an emotional breakdown. On my kitchen table, the Wedding Notebook, thick with ideas and information, glared at me. Beside it loomed a tall, unorganized stack of brochures from all the long-term care facilities we had visited.

"I have a ten o'clock appointment this morning!" I said in a panic, to no one. *But where? Does it have anything to do with the wedding? Is it for Steve's care? Something else entirely? Jesus, help me! I do not know what I am doing!*

I was completely disoriented and utterly overwhelmed. Deep breathing, caffeine, and prayer soon cleared my head, but I consequently lost my sense of taste for almost a year. Amazing what stress can do to you.

Toward the end of my final visit with Steve in the psychiatric hospital, he approached a staff member with a congenial smile and wrapped his arms around her in one of his harmless, signature bear hugs.

Abruptly pushing him away, she scolded, "Remember what we said about boundaries!"

It was time to get him out of there. Like our daughter, I also did not want Steve to feel defeated and small.

While I did not have a brain disease, I definitely had brain fog in the days surrounding Steve's move. Selecting the new memory care community with the welcoming, wide-open spaces, I completed more extensive paperwork and delivered a check for the first month's rent.

Upon reviewing Steve's history, the administrative staff recommended that he have a private room and showed Angie and me the one awaiting his arrival. It was nicely furnished, but the twin mattress was thin and the walls were bare, crying out for some TLC.

With Steve's comfort a priority, we first stopped at the nearest sleep store. As I purchased a more inviting twin-sized mattress for my husband, I ruminated on how different sleeping on this would be from the king-sized bed he was accustomed to. And I was painfully reminded that, for me, sleeping alone in that big bed at home was not temporary.

The immediate dilemma, however, was how to get the purchase into my car. Suddenly, a twin mattress didn't seem so small after all! What a sight Angie and I must have been driving down the road with that thing stuffed in my car like a sausage, protruding several feet out the back window. In order to make enough room, I thought for a moment that I might have to leave my sister on the curb!

Next I addressed the empty walls. Over Steve's new mattress and his favorite pillow—both covered by a colorful bedspread—I hung a sketch of his beloved Nora that I had given him for his birthday. Additional artwork from our house, family photos, and a few special coffee-table books with pictures of the western frontier endeavored to make it feel a bit more like home.

Outside each resident's door was a locked shadowbox to be filled by the resident or a family member. What was displayed in the shadowbox not only personalized each space, but it also helped the residents recognize the location of their rooms as they walked the hallways. For some individuals, their shadowbox was a shining reminder of a life well lived. For those in later stages of the disease, they were painful reflections of all that was lost. But each one told a story. Some held treasured dolls, delicate demitasse cups, or college sports memorabilia collected over a lifetime. Others paid tribute to veterans with military medals, armed services caps, and historic newspaper clippings. Almost all contained treasured family photos. I chose to fill Steve's with things representing what he held most dear—photos of the two of us and of Angela and Stephen, his certificate of honor from the Inn of Court, a tiny dog figurine atop a stack of miniature books, and a small wooden cross.

Two weeks before Angela's wedding, her father moved into his room in memory care. When I finally caught my breath, I informed our closest friends so they would understand why Steve would not be walking her down the garden aisle. Distressed by the news, one of them thoughtfully offered to sit with him at the facility during the ceremony. I gratefully declined, revealing, "Steve has lost almost all sense of time. If you don't tell him when Angela's wedding is and that it is taking place without him, he will have no idea."

And without him, it went on. There was a glaring, gaping hole next to me and in the entire evening, but we all did the best we could. Stephen lovingly walked his sister down the aisle, then took his place among the groomsmen. He joyfully welcomed the guests to the reception and made a poignant toast. With Angela in his arms, they transformed the traditional father-daughter dance into a memorable brother-sister one.

What a night! Our radiant daughter and her handsome new husband were the stars of the evening. Our loving son confidently performed his understudy role, becoming the fine young man we always knew he could be . . . That night, he knew it, too. And his own charming co-star and soon-to-be-fiancée, Kelly, was there waiting in the wings.

Their father would have been immensely proud. With the hole left by his absence, it was palpable to everyone what the Alzheimer's thief had taken away.

CHAPTER 17

Seventeen Months

For I am convinced that neither death nor life,
neither angels nor demons, neither the present nor the future,
nor any powers, neither height nor depth,
nor anything else in all creation,
will be able to separate us from the love of God
that is in Christ Jesus our Lord.

ROMANS 8:38–39 NIV

Step by prayerful step, we began moving through our newer reality. Before each visit to the memory care community, I asked God to bless our family time with Steve. I prayed that the Lord would shine his light on our children. And I thanked him continually for Angie, my unfailing champion, companion, and confidante.

While helping me select the right place for Steve, Angie had made me promise that I would not try to visit him every day.

Always concerned for my well-being, she did not want me to exchange one overwhelming set of caregiving responsibilities for another. I decided to make the twenty-minute drive three or four times a week.

Unsure of how Steve might react to the move, I arranged for non-emergency transport to take him from the psychiatric hospital to his new home. Once he was there, I waited four days for him to get settled in before I went to see him. Experts sometimes suggest a longer adjustment period, but I just couldn't wait anymore. Of course, Angie insisted on going with me, and I quickly agreed.

When we arrived, a large group of residents was gathered in the common area close to the reception desk. They were enjoying a musical performance, and most of them had their backs to us. I spotted Steve in the crowd.

As the music ended and he turned to leave, he suddenly saw me. Running toward me with open arms and a tear in his eye, he said repeatedly, "I'm sorry."

A million and one thoughts hit me all at once . . . *What on earth had they done to him at the psychiatric hospital? He has nothing to be sorry for! But if he is sorry, perhaps he really does understand what's happened and things will change. Does he truly even need to be here anyway?*

Those two words ripped me at the seams—so much so that I just couldn't tell the kids.

"I know, honey. I know. It's okay," was all I could say as we embraced and I cried too.

Angie continued to accompany me on many subsequent visits. Whenever I met with members of the staff, she was by my side. Angela and Stephen, Jody and Patti, Butch, a few of Steve's most loyal friends, Mary Claire, and Beckie—my dear friend since seventh grade—went to see him in the early weeks. Together, we gradually acclimated to his new environment. Of course, it was the most difficult for Steve.

During the transitional phase, I met Kimberly, whose official title was director of resident and family services. I'm not sure what was listed in her job description, but somehow she managed to be counselor, educator, advocate, head cheerleader, spiritual mentor, friend, colleague, mother, sister, daughter—whatever you or your loved one needed at the time. For our family, she became a guardian angel.

On one of our initial visits, she looked at Angie and me across the table and said, "I don't want to scare you, but . . ."

This was only the first of many times on our journey that I was on the receiving end of a sentence beginning with those words.

Kimberly continued, ". . . the average life expectancy of someone diagnosed with Alzheimer's before the age of sixty-five is approximately five years. Individuals with early-onset rarely live ten or more."

Already, it had been four years since Steve's diagnosis, and I had no idea how much time had passed since the actual onset.

"I'm not scared," I managed to say. "Thank you, I need the information."

One of the lessons Kimberly impressed upon frequent visitors was "big hellos, little goodbyes." Because Steve was generally happy to see us, the hellos were easy. As Kimberly predicted, the goodbyes were more difficult. Occasionally, we secretly were led out a side door if he attempted to follow us out the front. Staff members were masters at distraction with his new favorite soda, a freshly baked cookie, or a walk through the courtyard. I learned to preface my exit with a fiblet such as, "I have to go feed Nora," or "I need to get home before dark." Naturally, he wanted to come home with us, and it broke my heart to maintain my resolve that he should not. But the more confrontational he became during our departures, the more I knew I had made the right decision, difficult as it was. Not surprisingly, those behaviors made the children more reluctant to see him.

"Visiting was so painful. Really, all of it was," Stephen confided. "You know how you sometimes have to shake a container of breath mints really hard just to get one out? I felt like that container. Inwardly, I was shaken up so violently just to get that little emotional piece of me out there that it physically hurt every time I went to see him."

Invariably, Angela, Stephen, and I were experiencing yet another level of ambiguous grief—grieving the continued loss of their father, who was still very much alive. Although he and I had lived "alone together" for months, until his move, there was still perhaps some veiled hope that one day our lives would return to normal.

Added to my blender of emotions was the immense guilt I felt for placing him in long-term care layered on top of the guilt that had remained after moving my parents.

"I would worry about you if you didn't feel guilty," Kimberly told me. "It means you're human and that you care."

Honestly, it took me years to understand that by placing Steve in memory care when his needs exceeded my abilities, I was being the best caregiver I could be. Now we were not alone; we had care partners. Still, I had to work at accepting my own inadequacies in order to forgive myself.

Only a few weeks into his stay, I realized that Steve's dementia was considerably more advanced than that of many of the other residents, even though he was years younger than most and could still easily perform all the activities of daily living—eating, grooming, dressing, and so on. While his inability to complete another cognition exam came as no surprise to me, I was amazed to see how well others were doing cognitively. In one area of the building, residents worked jigsaw puzzles and played cards, bingo, and word games. Steve had long since lost the ability to do any of those things.

Members of the staff predicted he and another male resident, who dressed like a cowboy and was only a few years older, would become fast friends. Indeed, after spending some time with this gentleman, Steve asked me to bring him his own blue jeans and boots, which I readily did. In Steve's world, he *needed* those clothes. He also *needed* his newspapers and pens. He *needed* to "work" in Kimberly's office, which always had an open door and a couple of extra chairs. And he *needed* to watch soccer on TV, which sometimes presented a problem. Soccer was not always on the air, and most of the other residents did not care for it—especially the cowboy.

While Steve had grown accustomed to doing what he wanted to do when he wanted to do it, so had the cowboy. Alzheimer's is selfish. It does not know how to compromise. Thus, despite the staff's predictions, they did not become friends. In fact, it was quite the opposite.

"He is *not* a nice guy," Steve began commenting when we passed the cowboy in the hallway.

Funny, I thought, *he probably says the same thing about you!*

Because Steve was unwilling to share the common television area with others, it was not long before the activities director asked me to purchase a TV for his room. I did so, despite my doubts. He had been having plenty of difficulty with the TV remote at home; getting him acquainted, much less proficient, with a new one was going to be virtually impossible. And sure enough, a few short weeks after the television went up on the wall, it came back down. In frustration and anger, Steve had hurled the remote at the screen and broken it beyond repair.

As in so many senior living communities, the main dining room was a metaphor for middle school. It was important to choose your table wisely. Who you sat with determined your status in the community. Once your seat became "assigned," it stayed that way until someone else moved—in this case, to another dining area in the building or to a different facility. It astonished me how many things residents with early- to mid-stage dementia could not remember, and yet they always knew where to sit at mealtimes. This made it difficult for a newcomer to find a welcoming spot. Eventually, Steve managed to settle in alongside a sweet lady and an older gentleman who did not talk much.

The gentleman had a gadget that fascinated Steve, and he *needed* one for himself. Surprisingly, it was a flip phone, something I had not seen in years. As Steve had lost all ability to use his smart phone, I agreed that a less complicated flip phone could be a good idea. The store's sales representative preprogrammed it for me: I was number one, Angela was number two, and Stephen was number three. I even labeled the phone with our names and corresponding numbers to help Steve remember.

He was thrilled when I handed it to him and showed him how it worked. So thrilled, in fact, that one late night, he called me fifteen times in forty minutes.

When I wasn't visiting Steve, I was planning a wedding rehearsal dinner. A month after Angela and Matt's wedding, Stephen proposed to Kelly. Although they had known each other since kindergarten, they only started seriously dating after college. How fortunate I felt to have a son-in-law and soon-to-be daughter-in-law whom I admired and adored. They were the perfect matches for our children! As a bonus, I loved their families as well. And I knew how very blessed Steve and I were that they all planned to stay in Fort Worth.

As anyone who has taken on both roles can tell you, being Mother of the Groom is considerably easier and much less stressful than being Mother of the Bride. Nevertheless, with a May engagement and an October ceremony, there was much to get done. Once again, I was immensely grateful to have my sister, Angie, by my side, helping to plan every detail of the rehearsal dinner. I reveled in our time together as much as I valued her opinion. Excited about adding Kelly to our family, Angela was eager to assist as well.

Their wedding weekend is an emotional memory. Never did I imagine I would be giving the welcoming toast at our son's rehearsal dinner, but in his father's absence, the job fell to me. While toasting our newly joined families, Kelly's father eloquently paid homage to Steve just as Matt's dad had done six months earlier. How I wish they had gotten to know him pre-Alzheimer's!

Following a beautiful chapel ceremony, we celebrated under a cloudless sky that became illuminated by literal fireworks. It was breathtaking. But my breath was also knocked out of me by how lonely I felt in the crowd. This was not the first time, nor would it be the last.

Not long after the wedding, we faced our first holiday season without Steve at home. Surprisingly, it seemed more difficult for us than for him. When I raised the possibility of bringing him back to our house for Thanksgiving or Christmas, staff and family members adamantly discouraged the idea. For one thing, Steve was still extremely strong and very fast. What would happen if he became angry and aggressive at home? Could we catch up and find him if he wandered away? Might he refuse to get in the car for the return trip? What if it was impossible to persuade him to re-enter the facility's front door? Even if he willingly went back, we learned that the next two or three days could be extremely difficult for him and the staff as he readjusted to his surroundings and routine. I had to come to terms with the fact that, in this newer reality, nothing would ever be as it had been. We just had to make the best of it.

Fortunately, making the best of it was something Steve's memory care team did well. They festively decked the halls and common areas for every holiday from Valentine's through Christmas. Thoughtfully, they scheduled parties a few days prior to the actual holiday in order to allow families to continue personal traditions as much as possible. Not wanting Steve to feel alone or left out, one or two family members and I would join him at these celebrations. However, we soon discovered that the smaller gatherings we planned in the private dining room solely for our group were much more meaningful.

Buying gifts for Steve on these occasions, though, presented a conundrum. When new clothes were given, they had to be taken away for labeling before wearing. Picture books and framed family photos were certain to mysteriously disappear. Cologne was destined to be spilled. We came to understand that expensive gifts and fancy wrapping no longer held significance for Steve. A musical greeting card brought him more happiness than the latest best-selling novel once had. All that truly mattered was his pleasure in the moment.

For me, finding my own pleasurable moments was another thing altogether. Nothing about that first Christmas without my husband by my side seemed natural. Instead of singing holiday songs with the radio while running errands together in our car, I sang to him along with the other Sunshine Singers as we entertained at his facility. For the first time since Steve and I started dating, I went to parties by myself. There was no one handing me tissues as I watched *It's a Wonderful Life* for the fortieth time. Steve wasn't there to sip his favorite hot mulled cider with the kids or to watch them explore their Christmas stockings—a tradition we had continued well beyond their childhood. Somehow, we all muddled through, comforting ourselves with the knowledge that their dad was safe, comfortable, and content.

The minute I put my last ornament away, Angie called and urged, "Now let's get your house ready to put on the market!"

We both knew it was time. When Angela was in first grade, we had moved around the corner from our starter home to a larger house with a pool and a park-like backyard. We loved the lifestyle that came with it—from hosting birthday parties for throngs of gleeful children to gathering with our whole family during holidays to celebrating friends' milestones with wedding and baby showers.

Now, however, the massive upkeep and needed updates to this big old house were more than I could or should manage alone.

But where to begin? A shredding truck pulled into our driveway and obliterated countless boxes stuffed with unnecessary papers, some dating back to 1977, that had been living in our attic because Steve had refused to part with them. A junk truck made two trips to haul away unusable furniture, non-working appliances, and a well-worn Ping-Pong table from the basement. Angela and Stephen culled their belongings. Many days, I filled my car with clothing and household items to donate, slowly emptying our house of things we no longer needed. Finally, a few rooms were given a face-lift with a fresh coat of paint. Weeds were pulled and spring flowers planted.

Angie was by my side in March as I signed a contract listing our home with a realtor, just as she had been with me throughout the entire process.

As always, I continued visiting Steve at the memory facility as often as I could. Additionally, I began attending support group meetings there along with "lunch and learn" sessions that Kimberly regularly facilitated for residents' family members. Not only did I appreciate the expertise she shared, but it was also nice to learn what stories were behind the faces of others who frequently visited their loved ones.

One of the topics that captivated my interest was "anticipatory grief," addressing the emotional pain and "letting go" that can occur *before* an actual death. As Kimberly led us through the definition, symptoms, and benefits of anticipatory grief, she reassured us that it is extremely common in dementia patient caregivers. She also talked to us about "unfinished business" and the importance of "saying what needs to be said" at the end of life.

"I have had family members tell me that they can't find anything kind to say to their dying mother because she wasn't a good parent," Kimberly revealed. "I always tell them they *can* say, 'Mom, I know you did the best you could.' That way, they will have made peace and everyone is released from regret."

In my brain, I attended that session to prepare me for Steve's eventual death. The Holy Spirit knew better, however, and actually led me there to fill a more imminent need.

Later that spring, it became evident that my sister was extremely ill. She had hidden it from us, not wanting us to worry. Always in the past, whenever she was sick, she would stoically proclaim, "I'll power through it." And somehow, she always did. This time, tragically, she could not. The power just wasn't there.

We spent the summer of 2017 with Angie going in and out of the hospital. During her final stay in August—when it became apparent to the doctors that the measures they were taking to improve her condition were not working—they advised moving her into the hospice unit for her comfort and ours.

As soon as we got there, lessons from Kimberly's anticipatory grief session began to echo in my head. I reminded every visiting family member that although Angie's eyes were closed and she was unable to respond, she could hear every word they said. I told her daughter, my niece, Chandler, the story about the adult children who could only manage to tell their dying mother that they knew she had done the best she could.

"Your mom deserves so much more than that. You go in there and tell her that she has been the best mother in the world!" I urged.

The corners of her mouth lifted a bit as she nodded, knowing it was true.

Our beloved Angie passed during the night with her adored husband Butch and cherished daughter Chandler at her bedside. There are no words to describe the depth of my sorrow. I called Kimberly to request that the staff give Steve some extra attention because it would be many days before I could visit again.

Seventeen months earlier, we had been celebrating a wedding. Now we had a funeral to plan.

Speaking from her heart at the memorial service, Chandler embodied her mother's beautiful spirit and reminded us of Angie's selfless way of living:

> *She was always lifting up the work of others and rarely sought praise for her own. Her mind was constantly searching for ways to show others she was thinking of them. Not only would she do everything in her power to ease someone's burden, but she would do it in a way that went above and beyond anything that was expected.*

Angie's unselfish love helped carry me through the highs and lows of life and through the days surrounding her death. Soon after her service, she visited me in a dream and gently reassured me, "I don't cry." As God's word promises, she wanted me to know that she was free from pain and that there are no tears in heaven (Revelation 21:4). And I was comforted to know that she, our parents, and grandparents were having a joyful reunion.

Here on earth, however, as I entered yet another level of grief, I was not quite sure what to do with my own tears.

CHAPTER 18

Goodness, Grace Us!

Forget the former things; do not dwell on the past.
See, I am doing a new thing!
Now it springs up; do you not perceive it?
I am making a way in the wilderness
and streams in the wasteland.

ISAIAH 43:18–19 NIV

Saying the short goodbye to my sister while undergoing the long goodbye to my husband was almost more than I could bear. Selfishly, I ached with questions. How could she, the big sister I depended on, leave me when I already felt so desperately alone? How could I, as Angie would say, "power through" this new loss? On my own, I could not even begin to face it. Surely, only the divine comfort of the Holy Spirit got me through those days and the ones ahead . . .

The first time I visited Steve's care facility after Angie's death, I felt like a huge, essential piece of me was missing. While he and I sat side by side listening to the musical entertainment that day, I rested my head on his shoulder and he put his arm around me. Somehow, at that moment, I believe he knew I needed him more than he needed me. I remain grateful that he never asked about her. Just as with my mother after my father passed away, I would not have had the heart to tell him over and over again or the wherewithal to conjure up a fiblet.

As one day, one week, one month rolled into the next, I simply didn't know what to do with myself. Whenever a song by Angie's all-time favorite band, Chicago, came on the radio, I said aloud, "Hi, Angie. I miss you!" At Target, I averted my eyes from the "For Sister" section of the greeting card aisle in order to keep from crying. Every time I heard a bit of news that merited sharing or I craved a piece of advice, my first thought was to call her. And when I remembered that I couldn't, it was like losing my sister all over again. I searched for the few remaining safe places for my grief to land.

Morning, afternoon, and evening, I walked our dog, Nora, through the neighborhood . . . quite often in my pajamas. I didn't care who saw or what they thought. Normally, Nora was so excited about going out the front door that she would hardly stand still long enough for me to get the harness around her neck. Now she was so tired of the whole ordeal that she scurried off to hide whenever she saw me approaching with leash in hand.

Except to the few neighbors who might have taken notice of my attire, outwardly, I suppose, I appeared okay. I was "going through the motions," as they say. Inwardly, however, I numbed my

emotions in order to make it through each day. It was an uncon-
scious choice in the interest of self-protection. And while this
strategy did help ease the pain for a while, unfortunately, it also
dulled my joy.

On a Monday morning in November 2017, Angela called to ask
if she and Matt—both excellent cooks—could come over and make
dinner for me that evening. While the offer was a bit out of the ordi-
nary, it never occurred to me there was a hidden agenda. I readily
accepted. When they arrived, she handed me a small gift bag.

"Why are you giving me a present?" I asked.

"Just open it!" she replied with a smile.

Inside was a colorful children's board book about grandmother
wishes with an inscription in Angela's handwriting:

We're excited to tell you
We'll no longer be two,
In summer 2018,
Your first grandbaby is due!

Such glorious news! What wonderful timing! The circle of life
was beginning anew. I should have been jumping up and down with
glee. But my continuing sorrow over what *had been* rendered me
incapable of fully expressing my happiness for what was *to be*. My
subdued response is one of my lasting regrets, even though Angela
has continually and compassionately told me she understood.

As Steve's second winter in memory care approached, his daily
"uniform" of choice became khaki pants, a long-sleeved shirt
(sometimes three or more layered on top of one another), and a

fleece vest with deep pockets. On his feet were loafers or sneakers as he had lost the privilege of wearing cowboy boots after kicking in the door one too many times. Roaming from one bistro area to another, he overfilled his vest pockets with small bottles of water and pieces of string cheese from the refrigerators. Repeatedly, he requested Pepsi Colas—something he had never indulged in before—from the receptionist at the front desk. Drink one; put two in the pocket. No pack mule was ever as loaded down as my Steve!

He visited Kimberly's office frequently, either sitting in an empty chair, hovering over her as she worked, or using her pens to do his own "work" on the newspaper. She welcomed him always.

One afternoon, standing by the front desk as he often did, he repeatedly said the word "Pen!" The kind receptionist handed him one. He gave it back. "Pen!" he said again, a bit louder. This went on for quite some time, with Steve's frustration level clearly rising.

Kimberly passed by and tried to assess the situation. Although he was saying "pen," she pondered what he might really be asking for. From her office, she brought every kind of writing tool available—pens in various colors, pencils, markers, highlighters.

"Pen!" he shouted, angrily pushing them all away as quickly as they were offered.

"Steve," Kimberly said calmly as she regrouped her thoughts, "can you point to what you want?"

He pointed to the minifridge located behind the desk, where the sodas were kept. What he desperately wanted was a Pepsi, but he couldn't find the right word.

Steve's language difficulties mounted. His daily speech pattern started to include nonsensical phrases, such as "change water," which he would repeat over and over. Change what water? Where?

Why? From Kimberly, I learned that this kind of unintelligible, unorganized speech is common in dementia patients and is often referred to as "word salad." Whenever I visited, Steve repeated, "I want to go home for you," over and over. Although in my heart I believed that "home" had ceased to have the same meaning for him, it still broke a little each time I heard those words. I deeply wanted him to be able to come home *for* me and *with* me. But that was not our reality.

As I look back, the more difficult it became for Steve to express himself with his words or to understand mine, the more we unconsciously learned to communicate with our facial expressions and body language—always including a smile and a hug.

Now that he was no longer able to follow the action of his beloved soccer games on TV, Steve gravitated to watching movies about horses. On many visits, I sat with him as we drank Pepsi or enjoyed an ice cream sandwich in front of yet another showing of *My Friend Flicka*. Somehow, I never tired of it. It wasn't long before the word "horses" was popping up out of context and he was petting the horse sculpture hanging on the wall.

Soon it became clear that Steve could not remember if or when I visited. Of course, I did it for me, and to check in often on his care. But I also went because Kimberly reminded us, "He may not remember that you were here, but he will remember how you made him feel." Hopefully, the children and I—along with the other family members, friends, ministers, and church volunteers who visited now and then—made him feel happy, appreciated, and loved.

The Alzheimer's thief was devious in other ways too. Over time, my husband with the long-established morning routine forgot how to put in his contact lenses, how to shave, how to shower, and so much more.

"I don't know what that is," he said quizzically one afternoon as he pointed to an item on his nightstand. It was his must-have flip phone.

"No worries," I assured him. "If you don't want it, I'll just take it away."

We had turned another proverbial corner in the progression of the disease. And although there were dips in the road behind and ahead, there were high points as well.

Some bits of language that were not yet tossed in the word salad bowl were savored for a long time. "I love you!" Steve said easily and often, not only to me but also to his favorite members of the staff. Occasionally, I was on the receiving end of "You're so beautiful, Mama!" He affectionately began calling me "Baby Girl," a name that stuck and brought smiles to the care team's faces, as well as to both of ours. Many times, he proclaimed to them, "Kathe is my life!" In those few, precious words, not only was I reminded of his devotion to me but also of my profound responsibility as his wife.

On many visits, I would search the halls for my husband only to find him happily engaged in chair kickball, patiently attempting to paint a flower on canvas, or outside on the patio enjoying an ice cream social. The activities staff truly did their best to engage Steve in every possible way.

I also learned to bring my own brand of entertainment. Sometimes it was in the form of food—a yummy, chopped barbeque sandwich here or a delectable piece of Black Forest cake there. Regularly, I took one of the scrapbooks I'd made following our trips to Alaska, Italy, and Hawaii to share with my old travel companion.

It didn't matter how many times we looked at them—for Steve, each time was like the first. In addition, I created a special photo book, featuring pictures of his family spanning six decades. It included some priceless, old black-and-white photos, as well as newer color ones of Steve with his brother, parents, grandmother, our children, and me. The cover read *Steve Goodwin: This Is Your Life*, and every time I showed it to him, I guarded it with my own. It was too precious to lose.

Our big shaggy dog was a frequent visitor with me to Steve's community. How he enjoyed proudly walking her around the courtyard and through the hallways, telling anyone who would listen, "This is Nora. She's a labradoodle," until he couldn't quite get those words out anymore. This pet I had initially resisted became an unofficial therapy dog for him, for many of the residents, and even for the staff. At home, she kept me from being quite so alone . . . even though she still loyally slept by Steve's side of the bed.

Late one afternoon as dinnertime was approaching at the memory care center, Steve, Nora, and I settled in at a table on the edge of the dining room. Dogs were no longer allowed in the dining areas because residents had constantly fed them from their plates and made them unhealthily fat. Although the rule was initiated to benefit the facility-owned dogs, it applied to residents' and visitors' pets as well. Steve was particularly flustered this day, and I wasn't quite ready to leave him. I figured that if he, Nora, and I were going to disregard the rules, we would do so on the perimeter and be as discreet as possible.

"You can't have that dog in here," a gruff voice came from two tables away. It was a resident's husband who visited for several hours each and every day. I marveled at his devotion. Not only had I never seen his wife smile, but the effects of her dementia had made her most unpleasant to be around as well.

"I'm sorry. I know," I responded. "But could you please cut us a little slack this once? We're having a bit of a rough day."

"Humph," he scoffed as he shook his head. "Every day is a rough day for us."

I knew it was true. Years of thankless caregiving had taken its relentless toll and shaken every piece of happiness right out of him. My heart hurt for them both.

On good days and bad, music became a magnet for Steve, attracting him wherever and whenever he could hear it playing. My husband, who once upon a time had very little rhythm, somehow found his feet and made every corridor his dance floor. Savvy caregivers even danced him into the shower on days he was reluctant to bathe. When I visited, he twirled me around and around until I was almost too dizzy to stand. We stepped and swayed to Elvis and Sinatra impersonators, saxophone soloists, singing cowboys, Motown playlists, and more. If I was not there, laughter erupted as he danced with willing members of the staff.

"Has he always loved to dance?" they asked.

"No way! I used to have to drag him onto the dance floor," I chuckled.

One afternoon during the Christmas season, I was seated with Steve and about twenty other residents, waiting in anticipation for a musical performer who never arrived. So I stood up, pretended to have the other Sunshine Singers around me, and enthusiastically began leading the group in simple holiday sing-alongs like "Jingle Bells" and "Joy to the World." I was thrilled most were smiling and participating the best they could!

After our "Rudolph the Red-Nosed Reindeer" once more went down in history, two young women on the activities staff showed up with a karaoke machine. That was my cue to again take my chair beside Steve. But what those staffers did next will baffle me forever. They played "The Twelve Days of Christmas." Some of the best minds around cannot remember how many "maids a-milking" or "lords a-leaping" are in that song. How could individuals with dementia possibly be expected to follow along? Not surprisingly, the energy in the room shifted.

Of all the music throughout the year, however, Steve's favorite was played on Sundays. Every week, two brothers ministered to the memory care community. They typically arrived one at a time, and each of them immediately embraced Steve and his penchant for stealing the spotlight. One brought a guitar, incredible energy, and an infectious smile. When he played and sang gospel music, Steve was standing right beside him, clapping his hands, stomping his feet, and doing his best to sing along. The other brother flourished at the piano and often brought his wife, who joined him in harmonious duets, as well as their adorable toddler son. Even then, it was difficult to keep Steve in his chair. Along with their uplifting music, these two Christian servants delivered short, simple messages of faith, hope, and love to everyone in attendance. It was good to go to church with my husband again.

Spring arrived as a whisper. With the change of season, I dutifully drove to the cemetery to replace the faded winter poinsettias with vibrant, artificial pink geraniums. After carefully arranging them in the vases, I paused in suspended disbelief at Angie's headstone. As I reflected on all that was and pined for all that might have been,

I heard a voice clearly speak to me in a tone and manner that was unmistakably my sister's.

"Go home, Kathe," she said matter-of-factly.

Of course, that would be Angie! Still as selfless as ever, she did not want me spending any more time there mourning her.

As usual, I did what she asked. And I did a little bit more. After taking my house off the market for several months, I re-listed it with a new energy and commitment to sell. I updated my legal documents, granting Angela and Stephen durable and medical powers of attorney. And I revised my will not only in the interest of our children and future grandchildren but also to ensure that Steve's needs would be met if he outlived me.

In June, a blessed bundle of boy joy entered the world and filled my heart with a new kind of love. Angela and Matt's baby, Hays, was born, and I became a doting "Kacky." What a busy Kacky I was! When Angela returned to work in September, I began a Tuesday–Thursday routine of picking Hays up from daycare and watching him for the afternoon. It was a newfound pleasure, as well as a new commitment.

Then came a weekend none of us will ever forget. My niece, Chandler, had previously been a sales representative for a women's clothing company and she had a backlog of clothes she wanted to sell. They were cute, comfortable, and surely marketable. She just needed to get them out there! After agreeing to have a Saturday afternoon sale in my home, I emailed friends and placed flyers on neighbors' doors while Chandler handled the social media outreach. I shifted furniture to accommodate the hoped-for crowds, set up full-length mirrors in the living room, and brought the rolling clothes rack up from the basement. All that was missing was Chandler, the clothes, and all those buyers. Nestling into the notion that I was doing something nice for my niece, I slept well Friday night ... until Saturday morning awakened me early with a vengeance. Jolts of thunder, bolts of lightning, and torrents of rain, rain, and more rain.

"The clothes will be totally ruined if I try to transport them to your house," Chandler lamented over the phone. "There is no way we can have the sale."

She was right, of course. I emailed my friends, informing them of the cancellation. I put a sign on the front door in case anyone actually braved the weather and showed up. And I opened the door to the basement to return the rolling rack ...

What was that sound? I had never heard it before. It sounded like rushing water. To my horror, water—a river of murky, muddy water—was gushing into the basement from under and around the door leading to the exterior stairway. So much rain over so little time was more than the outside drain could handle. The basement had not flooded in fifteen years! And never like this!

What to do? When we had experienced small basement floods before, Steve was there and we had figured it out together. Now I was on my own ... It was a "Help me, Jesus!" moment.

But "Please help me, Jody!" was what I said on the frantic phone call to my brother. By the time he and his son-in-law arrived, the water over the exterior drain was knee-deep, and it was still raining buckets. To this day, I do not know how they did it. Something about using a hose as a siphon ... All I know is the water stopped spewing into the basement, they were drenched from head to toe, and I am forever grateful.

Next I had to get the floodwater out of the basement. I did what I could, moving furniture and rugs and sweeping water into interior drains. Needless to say, with a rain of nearly biblical proportions (God forbid it should have lasted forty days and nights!), I was not the only homeowner in the city needing assistance from a water damage restoration company. Thankfully, the first one I called responded to my desperate plea. They came. They saw. They turned on their water extraction and drying equipment.

At eleven o'clock that Saturday night, after mopping for what seemed like hours, I was on my hands and knees scrubbing residual dirt off the basement tile floor. Why didn't I wait until the next day to tackle that filthy, exhausting chore? Because my realtor had scheduled an open house for Sunday afternoon.

One definition of grace is "the influence or spirit of God operating in humans to regenerate or strengthen them." I thank God for showering us with his grace that weekend. We needed it in abundance. And while I did not immediately get a contract on my house, it was not long before I did.

CHAPTER 19

Stepping Out

For we walk by faith, not by sight.

2 CORINTHIANS 5:7 RSV

As autumn generally does, October put renewed zest in my step.

At Chandler's suggestion, she and I shared a long weekend in the charming little town of Fredericksburg in the Texas Hill Country. We bonded more deeply in recalling cherished memories of her mother, shared scrumptious meals together, and began our Christmas shopping with cheerful eagerness. It was a welcome and wonderful distraction for me on many levels, especially because I was nervously anticipating the sale of my house.

After breakfast on Monday morning, Chandler and I packed up my car and began the four-hour drive back to Fort Worth in the rain, with more rain to come. We were glad we left when we did. As we headed north, it was literally flooding behind us. It seemed impossible that she and I again were experiencing such an aggressive downpour!

At home, however, Angela was experiencing a welcome outpouring of support for the team she was forming to honor her father in the 2018 Walk to End Alzheimer's. Not only did "Steve's Stars" vastly exceed her fundraising goal, but she also inspired many with this deeply personal story she posted on the Alzheimer's Association website:

> My father, Steve, was diagnosed with early-onset Alzheimer's at the age of sixty-one. He was a prominent attorney, an attentive father, a loving husband, and a fiercely independent man. Alzheimer's has taken a lot from me, but it is nothing compared to what it has taken from my father.
>
> A brilliant man with a vast vocabulary first lost the ability to find his words. He stumbled to pick from his brain the correct word to fit a certain situation. He then had difficulty following along with the legal conversations at work and accomplishing the day-to-day tasks at home that came so easily before. This was followed by a long and arduous journey during which he lost much of his learned mental and physical abilities and saw drastic changes to his temperament and behavior.
>
> I have watched a small piece of the man I once knew leave him each day for the past eight years. He currently lives a simple existence at a memory care facility in south Fort Worth, visited often by my mom and his sweet "therapy dog" Nora.
>
> I have heard this disease referred to as "the long goodbye." I have been saying goodbye to my father for years. I miss him every day. I miss asking him for advice. I miss crying on his shoulder. I miss leaning on him when I felt that no one else was on my side. I miss long talks that I am sure now would be filled with parenting advice and commiseration as

well as a few "I told you so" moments from the man who raised me. I miss hearing him speak in full sentences. I miss hearing him say my name.

I wish I had a better memory. My brain cannot recall what it was like when he was scolding me as a teenager or when he told me he loved me as a child. So much of what I remember is coming from old home videos and dreams that are only partially based in reality.

I was cheated out of the experience of walking down the aisle with my dad. My husband was cheated out of a father-in-law to share his love of history and books. My brother and I deserve an adult relationship with him. My mom deserves a partner to share her life with, to make decisions with, and to travel with. My son deserves a grandfather who can play with him, watch him grow, and say his name.

But instead, here we are.

I consider myself lucky, however, because I can still hug my dad today. I visited him a few days ago, and he hugged my son and made faces as Hays held his finger. All is not lost, but all is not as it should be. Alzheimer's has taken a lot from my family, but it has also given us a lot. My father dances with my mom when it was hard to entice him to the dance floor before. We have gained perspective, humility, and understanding.

I truly am my daddy's girl, and I hope someday other children do not have to experience the heartache my family and I have felt. Please consider walking or donating to honor my father and those like him who need us to fight their fight.

How exceedingly proud I was of our daughter. How energized I was to join her, our family, and friends in the Walk to End Alzheimer's. How violently ill I was when I awakened in the wee hours of that October Saturday morning. The twenty-four-hour stomach virus that Angela had endured the day before had now caught up with me. I don't know how she physically managed to participate in the walk at all, let alone alternate with Matt in pushing Hays in his stroller. To my overwhelming disappointment, I was only able to walk feebly from bed to bathroom and back on repeat that day. (Fortunately, our family was able to walk together in honor of Steve the following year.)

Our fortieth wedding anniversary was soon approaching. For decades, I had looked forward to that milestone. Steve and I had always wanted to see France together and I'd dreamed of celebrating our fortieth on a rooftop in Paris. Or perhaps we would fly to San Francisco, where we spent our honeymoon and tenth anniversary. Or maybe we would simply return to our favorite Dallas hotel for a romantic weekend staycation.

"But instead," as Angela so honestly wrote, "here we are"—in the common dining area of a long-term memory care facility, where Steve is a resident.

In these surroundings, reminders of our lost dreams for the future were inescapable. To make the best of things, I brought cake from our favorite bakery, a miniature bottle of sparkling wine, and our cherished wedding photo album—a tribute to a more innocent time. As usual during my visits, I tried simply to be present in the moment and not to think too much or too hard. But on this once-in-a-lifetime day, my mind and my heart echoed, *My choice is to love Steve and honor my vows, to be strong and trust in the Lord, and to thank God for all that we have been given.* Hearing my silent prayer, the Lord soon gave me an unexpected anniversary gift.

"Mom, are you sitting down?" Angela asked excitedly over the phone.

"Not yet, but I will," I answered. "What's up?" Clearly, she had some big news to share.

What followed was the story of how she had just discovered my long-lost wedding ring. It was hiding in the bottom of a box containing a Christmas angel, which I had given her exactly a year before. Somehow it had slipped off my finger without my noticing at the time. That luminous angel was truly a guardian! I was thrilled to know that my ring finger, which had felt quite naked for twelve months, would soon be dressed again.

Later that day, as I slipped my wedding band back on, it was a bittersweet reminder that I, in so many ways, was married to an absent spouse.

On November 19, the day after our anniversary, I closed on the purchase of a new house exactly one month after selling our previous home. Virtually everything in me and everyone around me told me this was the right thing to do. Still, there was that little piece of me that felt like a traitor. This is not what Steve would have wanted. On the other hand, I believed he also would not want me to stay alone in a home that overly stretched me in every way. The contract on the old house allowed me to live there until after the first of the new year. That gave me needed time to make some desired changes to my new residence before I moved in. It also provided me the opportunity to host extended family for one final Thanksgiving and to celebrate one last intimate Christmas in our family home.

Twenty-three years of memories were within those walls and fences. I reflected on our first Easter when we had no furniture in our living room but had the best egg hunt ever in our big new backyard. There was a carefree summer of fireflies and friendly toads that the kids aptly named King Kong, Pee Wee, Romeo, and Juliet. We celebrated Angie's Fourth of July birthday around the pool with a legendary watermelon seed-spitting contest. I thought of our romping golden retriever puppy, who quickly stole our hearts, as well as Stephen's socks, and whom we comforted during thunderstorms through the years. Etched in my mind were myriad school science, history, and leprechaun-trap projects that repeatedly got shifted to the end of the kitchen table at dinnertime. But cherished Christmas memories were the hardest to leave behind—with Nat King Cole on the stereo, the kids in matching pajamas, and Steve on the other side of the video camera, capturing every precious moment.

There is a reason why Geoffrey Chaucer wrote, "All good things must come to an end."

Time to pack up the tinsel and wipe away the tears. Time to begin making new memories in a new space. Time to step out.

How was I to know that Steve would soon be stepping out as well . . . and what new leaps of faith we would be compelled to take?

CHAPTER 20

Wings and Prayers

Have I not commanded you? Be strong and courageous.
Do not be afraid; do not be discouraged,
for the Lord your God will be with you wherever you go.

JOSHUA 1:9 NIV

Looking forward with hope, I began the new year by writing in a brand-new journal.

January 1, 2019

The first page in a new chapter as I soon move into a new home after twenty-three years. I try to focus on the positives and not reflect too much on the past.

January 2, 2019

Began new daily devotional book with the new year. It reminds me that Jesus is my joy regardless of any life circumstances.

January 3, 2019

I continually pray for guidance, for comfort, and for strength as Steve went to the emergency room today for combative behaviors that could not be calmed and was admitted to the hospital with 101-degree fever.

The unexpected call came on my cell phone that afternoon while I was at Target checking things off my shopping list.

"We have been unable to calm Steve down," the new administrative director at the memory care facility informed me. This was the first call I had ever received from her, and there was a disconcerting background noise in the gaps between her words.

"I'll be right there!" I exclaimed.

"No, it's too late," she dispassionately responded. "The paramedics are already here. What hospital do you want them to take him to?"

And just like that our boat was adrift again. It really was the perfect storm.

For months, numerous staff changes—from the top down—had been happening at Steve's facility. Kimberly had left in June. Many of my other favorite staff members, including those who knew, understood, and communicated best with Steve, were gone.

The remaining few to whom Steve responded well had taken time off over the holidays. As his behaviors began to escalate, the prevailing response was to increase his medication, time and time again. Whenever someone called to inform me about a new drug regimen, I asked a few questions and gave my consent. In hindsight, I should have done more research and not been so quick to approve, but I reasoned that the medical professionals knew much more than I did. When the last drug cocktail did not have the desired calming effect, they introduced a new medication into his system. No one was prepared for what happened next . . . If Steve's recent behaviors had resembled choppy waters, they soon became raging seas.

But just as Jesus calmed the storm, the Lord truly works in mysterious ways.

Steve was safe in the hospital while medical personnel there helped him work his way back to baseline. Because there was not a single doctor, not even a neurologist, in the hospital who specialized in dementia-related care, they arranged for us to have weekday teleconference calls with outside psychiatrists. By "outside," I mean way outside—several states away. If one psychiatrist had an emergency before or during our scheduled visit (which happened more than once), we started all over with another the following day. Steve could not answer their questions, of course, so I did—including the one about bipolar disorder. Just as I knew, they agreed that was an erroneous diagnosis that never should have been put on his records.

Mostly, they reviewed how he was responding to ongoing changes in his medication. That was a good thing. One day he slept, and the next he was hostile. One day he and I danced in the hallway, and the next he was too unsteady on his feet to take even a few steps.

I felt very alone in that big hospital ... except that I wasn't. I see now how God surrounded me with love in those uncertain days. Although it introduced a further level of grief for the children to see their dad so very lost in that hospital bed, they visited and brought dinner. Mary Claire, my devoted friend, spent an extremely rough, emotional day with me, going in and out of his room and making sure I ate something at lunchtime. As usual, she provided nourishment for my soul, as well as for my body. Remarkably, she and I were able to attend Chandler's thirtieth birthday dinner that evening, thanks to an insightful nurse who arranged for Steve to have a round-the-clock hospital sitter. That one decision alleviated enormous strain on the hospital staff and on our family. I was in the midst of angels ... and more were hovering nearby.

With each new dawn of Steve's hospital stay, I was losing confidence and trust in his memory care facility. The new director of resident and family services never once called to check on us. I am fairly certain that was part of her job, as we were the very definition of "resident" and "family."

After some interrogation, the facility's administrative director informed me that Steve would be required to spend time in a psychiatric hospital before being allowed to return to his old room. To my mind, the only saving grace in her earlier, unsettling call to the paramedics was that I got to choose the hospital for my husband this time. Never again would I send the man I loved, a man living with Alzheimer's disease, to a psychiatric hospital.

When I talked on the phone with his physician from the facility, she told me she *had not* recommended a psychiatric stay for Steve.

The administrative director told me that she *had*. Someone was not telling the truth.

"I don't want to scare you, but . . ." Steve's physician began. There were those words again! My heart was in my throat. How was this sentence going to end?

". . . when behaviors erupt in this manner, it is often a signal that the disease is turning a corner, moving into a more advanced stage," she continued. Okay, that wasn't great. But that I could deal with.

"Doctor, right now, the only thing you can say that will scare me is that there isn't any place for Steve to go," I responded.

I prayed at home. I prayed in the car. I prayed at the hospital. "Lord, please show me what is best for Steve. Lord, please tell me who to turn to. Lord, should I call Kimberly?"

When the Lord answered yes, I picked up my phone and left this message: "Kimberly, this is Kathe Goodwin. You know Steve, and you know me. We really need a friend right now."

And what a friend she turned out to be. After she left Steve's memory care facility six months prior, the community had never felt the same. How we missed her smile and compassion, her knowledge and experience, her wisdom and faith.

Now Kimberly was in a new position at the James L. West Center for Dementia Care, a faith-inspired, not-for-profit organization with an outstanding reputation. I knew the center well; it is where my parents spent their last few months.

During our conversation, I did most of the talking while Kimberly listened. I knew she was listening not only with her ears, but also with her heart.

Finally, she said, "If this is what you want, I think we can find a place for Steve here."

With a sigh of relief and a prayer of gratitude, I picked up my journal and pen once again:

January 12, 2019

I have not written in the last few days because Steve's hospital stay, arranging his move into the James L. West Center (which happened today with Jody's help!), and my upcoming move have consumed me. You know you've had a tough week when doing laundry and paying bills seems like a vacation.

As my January 25 moving date drew closer, I juggled visiting Steve at the West Center and helping him adjust to his new surroundings, packing boxes, planning an estate sale, babysitting Hays, and remodeling parts of my new home. When I introduced myself to the energetic young mother next door, she exclaimed, "I've been praying for a good neighbor!" I had been too!

A few busy weeks after I moved in, Hays spent the night with me. We had enjoyed visiting his grandfather "Stevie" in his new home several days earlier. Now I had a "therapy baby," as well as a therapy dog. On this night, however, Hays had a miserable cold, which naturally he shared with me. Long after he fully recovered, I was still sniffling, coughing, and dragging about.

I dragged myself right into Bluebonnet Bakery, a small neighborhood café, for some hot soup. After placing my order at the counter, I said hello to a friend and between coughs informed her about Steve's move.

Once I settled into my booth, a woman sitting alone at a nearby table caught my eye. She had no food or drink, and no one else seemed to be paying any attention to her. But for some reason, she mesmerized me. For one, she was beautiful. Neither young nor old, she had flawless, glowing skin with just the right amount of makeup in all the right places. Her golden blonde hair was pulled up in a perfect twist with loose tendrils framing her face. She had a quiet air of confidence. I found myself staring.

As she clasped her hands together and bowed her head in prayer, I wondered what might be going on in her life or in the life of someone she loved. What was she praying about? Who was she praying for?

Eventually, I refocused my gaze and my attention to my soup, remembering that I probably should eat it before it got cold.

Unexpectedly, I felt a soft touch on my arm. I looked up to see the woman standing beside me. When she began to speak, I interrupted, babbling an apology about staring because I loved her hairstyle or some such nonsense.

She waited patiently for me to finish before speaking in a clear and soothing voice. Then she walked out the door with effortless grace. I wish I had followed her. I do not know whether she drove away in an SUV or flew on heavenly wings. What I do know is that I was touched by an angel who had been praying for me, for Steve, for our family. This is what she said:

"God wants me to tell you that everything is going to be okay."

CHAPTER 21

Coasting

And my God will supply every need of yours
according to his riches in glory in Christ Jesus.

PHILIPPIANS 4:19 RSV

Having endured the unbelievably steep slopes and incredibly sharp turns of the past few months, I welcomed the day our roller coaster seemed to slow down from "roller" to "coast" mode. Finally, for once, it really did feel as if "everything is going to be okay."

For Steve, the James L. West Center for Dementia Care was exactly the right place at the right time. He transitioned much more easily than I did. I missed the large, open spaces and the easily accessible courtyard of his former home. Here, he was confined to a small third-floor wing or "house," as they called it, and we had to ride an elevator to get even close to the outdoor areas. None of that seemed to bother Steve.

Each individual house bore the name of a river running through Texas. His was Pecos, and it was known unofficially as the unit for residents struggling with disruptive behaviors. While Steve's aggressive outbursts had definitely lessened in intensity and frequency following his hospital stay, I understood why he was placed there. Like the other men in this house, Steve could still be unpredictable. Blessedly, the experienced care team members—experts at intervening, de-escalating, and distracting—immediately took him under their wing.

It was only a few weeks before I realized that Steve's unanticipated hospital stay—as painful as it had been—was just the kick in the pants I needed to move him to this distinct environment. The Lord had given me a swift wake-up call.

When he arrived at the West Center, Steve weighed less than 140 pounds. His ribs protruded, his stomach was concave, and his pants—now a size thirty-two waist—were loose. He was "scary-thin." In my ignorance, I had assumed this was yet another aspect of his stage of Alzheimer's that couldn't be helped.

Soon after the move, however, Steve began to put on weight. The medical team added an appetite stimulant and began giving him calorie-laden shakes. Because his attention span was extremely short, he frequently would leave the dining table and his plate mid-meal to pace the hallway. Thus, for a long time, his food intake had gone down as his physical activity went up. And we had all just accepted it. But here, the caregivers routinely followed him up and down the hall with a sandwich in hand, walking alongside him until he had eaten it all. Then they chased him down with a cookie! At this point, it really didn't matter where the calories were coming from so long as he was eating.

"We can't get pants on Steve!" a sweet, concerned nurse told me over the phone several months into his stay.

Immediately, my mind jumped to his behavioral issues, and I imagined that he was being oppositional and resisting getting dressed. "I'm so sorry," I said. "Sometimes I can help. I'll be right there!"

She chuckled. "No, it's not that. I mean we *literally* can't get pants on him. They are all too small!"

By this time, Steve had outgrown every pair of his old and new pants in three sizes. He weighed 180 pounds, a weight he had never allowed the scale to reach at any time in our marriage. I went shopping at Walmart.

In other ways too, it seemed like the holes in our safety net were being mended. The much smaller space at the West Center, which I initially found restrictive, seemed to comfort Steve. At this point in his disease, the fact that he didn't have as many places to wander was actually a plus for him. And with only a few rooms along one short hallway, it was easier for me to find him when I visited.

"He's playing Goldilocks today," a caregiver often would greet me with a grin. Together we'd search several rooms to discover which resident's bed Steve had deemed "just right" on that particular afternoon. It never took long.

As I got to know the staff members who worked in Steve's house, I came to respect, admire, and genuinely like them. More than anything, I appreciated their servant's hearts, which prompted them to do indescribably difficult jobs day after day.

"Yours is a higher calling," I reminded them each time their invisible halos came into my view.

And as they got to know Steve, they came to genuinely like him too. "You know, Steve's our *favorite!*" more than one caregiver whispered in my ear.

Indeed, Steve freely shared his smiles, hugs, and I-love-yous with the entire care team. It wasn't long before I was telling them "I love you" as well.

Music continued to bring him joy, even in this new environment. A cheerful music therapist visited the houses often. Keeping rhythm as she played guitar and sang "Twist and Shout," Steve twisted while shaking maracas, and he shouted, "Ah, ah, ah!" while beating a drum. Whenever a Motown tune came over the speakers, his enthusiastic caregivers stood in line for their turn to dance with him. During mealtimes, the mellow notes of a saxophone or piano recording could be heard in the background. Like many long-term care facilities, the West Center was on the list of venues where the Elvis and Sinatra impersonators, as well as several other local musical acts, played regularly. Steve happily alternated between sitting and dancing throughout their performances . . . until his restlessness began prompting him to exit early. Although I had retired from the Sunshine Singers when I started regularly babysitting Hays, it was good to know they were still entertaining here as well.

At our prior memory care community, the cold void created by Kimberly's absence had been tangible. The quilt of educational opportunities and the warm blanket of tightly knit support groups had simply unraveled. I missed them immensely. Now that she had joined forces with the West Center, however, she was using her skills to enhance and expand their already existing programs. Once again, I was inspired to learn from experts face-to-face and to exchange thoughts and feelings across a table with others who, like me, were making their way through an unwanted journey with no road map. Here were new faces with new stories of lives and loved ones to share. And as Kimberly encouraged me to share ours, I began to feel God place an unexpected calling on my heart.

Little did I or anyone else know then that we were coasting into an unimaginably sharp bend.

CHAPTER 22

A New Kind of Thief

We are hard pressed on every side, but not crushed;
perplexed, but not in despair;
persecuted, but not abandoned;
struck down, but not destroyed.

2 CORINTHIANS 4:8–9 NIV

The year 2020 began much as 2019 had ended, with our little corner of the world—although forever flipped on its axis—blessed to be living out some long-held hopes and dreams.

At their annual family Christmas dinner, Stephen and Kelly had excitedly announced they were expecting their first baby in June. As we welcomed the new year, I joyfully looked forward to having another grandson to shower with love.

In late February, Angela, Stephen, and I traveled to New York City for the eagerly anticipated wedding of a close family friend. We took advantage of our time together there by seeing *Ain't Too Proud* and *Mean Girls* in sold-out Broadway theaters, dining elbow-to-elbow with hungry patrons in a famed delicatessen, and enjoying a guided tour of Brooklyn that included subway rides and walks through historic neighborhoods.

On March 7, Chandler married Carter, a wonderful young man from Fort Worth, in a small outdoor wedding. As Butch walked his beautiful daughter down the aisle, we could sense Angie's loving, motherly presence and pride. Stephen (who was ordained online) officiated the ceremony, which was followed by a festive reception for family and friends on the patio of a nearby Mexican restaurant. The happy newlyweds flew to France for a week-long honeymoon the next day.

Meanwhile at the West Center, things seemed mostly status quo. From the top down, there had been few staff changes, which was reassuring after our previous experience—especially since I had grown so fond of everyone there. Although Steve was declining, the progression of his Alzheimer's appeared to have plateaued somewhat. While I was still receiving occasional calls about altercations between him and a few of the other residents, Steve was now seldom the instigator. More often than not, he was acting out in retaliation or in an attempt to protect himself.

He still habitually roamed the house, but his gait was not quite as quick. On one visit, a care team member approached me and said he had been repeating a woman's name as he paced the hallway.

"Who is Wanda?" she asked.

"I have no idea!" I replied with a laugh. Who could know *what* was going on in his brain or *what* he was trying to say?

The dietary staff had modified his meals to include mostly finger foods since he had completely lost the ability to use dining utensils, but he could still quite capably feed himself. Oddly enough, my husband, who had been right-handed his entire life, now ate with his left.

My favorite time to visit Steve was during lunch. For some reason, I believed my presence alone would be enough to entice him to sit through an entire meal at the table. Sometimes I was right; others I was wrong. On one particular day, I enjoyed the challenge of urging him to finish his baked chicken and green beans before eating his second piece of chocolate cake. It was Tuesday, March 10. When I said goodbye to Steve that afternoon, the possibility that I wouldn't be allowed in the same building with my husband for almost seven agonizing months never even crossed my mind.

The next day, I, along with the other residents' primary contacts, received a cautionary email regarding visits. And on Friday, March 13, the James L. West Center for Dementia Care firmly closed its doors to any and all visitors. A new kind of thief had arrived on the scene. Its name was COVID-19.

As the world was being engulfed by the global pandemic, changes began happening at breakneck speed.

Chandler and Carter were robbed of the final days of their honeymoon in a frantic but ultimately successful attempt to return safely home.

In town for Chandler's wedding, Butch's lovely girlfriend, Elsie—whom he had known since growing up in West Texas—couldn't return to her home in Kansas for months.

On the last day of his ski trip in Deer Valley, Utah, Stephen heard an announcement that the mountain's lifts and trails were completely shutting down just as he turned in his rental equipment.

For the first time in forty-three years, Steve and I were pulled apart on his birthday.

When schools didn't reopen after spring break, Angela and Matt quickly became adept at teaching elementary art and high school geography over the internet with a toddler in the room.

We learned how to zoom with a capital Z.

Kelly and Stephen's long-anticipated baby shower morphed into a virtual celebration with absent friends sending gifts to their house. It was soon followed by a drive-by "Diaper Dash" where packs of diapers were tossed out of car windows onto their lawn.

All theaters went dark, squashing plans Mary Claire and I had made to share *Beautiful: The Carole King Musical* with her husband (as we had with Steve in New York) at the Bass Performance Hall in Fort Worth. Intuitively, she sat down at her sewing machine and began making face masks before I ever realized I would need one.

Traveling, sporting events, concerts and festivals, houses of worship, stores, restaurants, hair and nail salons, gyms, even doctors' and dentists' offices shut down in an effort to stop the spread of the coronavirus. Anything that was considered "non-essential" closed its doors. All large gatherings, including graduations, weddings, and funerals, were either canceled or postponed. It was like living in a never-ending episode of *The Twilight Zone*. We actually formed *pods*.

"If COVID doesn't kill me, loneliness will," I told Angela and Stephen during the early weeks of the shutdown.

Already, I had friends who were barred from seeing their children and grandchildren in the hope of keeping everyone protected from the virus. Because I lived alone, I knew that would either drive me literally crazy or sink me into a deep depression. Neither were good choices. Blessedly, the kids agreed our immediate pod would consist of them, Matt, Hays, Kelly, baby Goodwin, and me. Of course, they formed pods with their in-laws as well. Together we pledged to be vigilant in protecting ourselves with masks and frequently washed and sanitized our hands on the rare occasions we had to venture out. Whoever thought that a trip to the grocery store in the modern-day U.S. would be considered hazardous duty? But we went scavenging in search of food, highly coveted toilet paper, and disinfecting wipes. And then we used those wipes to scrub our bags, boxes, cans, and plastic containers, as well as all our counters, doorknobs, phones, and remotes.

Quickly, we learned that—much like Alzheimer's—the COVID-19 thief was relentless and non-discriminatory. But unlike dementia, it was contagious—extremely so. Although most deaths and more serious cases came to the elderly or those with pre-existing medical conditions, no one was exempt. It cruelly took lives, and as one month of closures rolled into the next, it ripped away livelihoods as well.

At 3:00 p.m. on Friday, April 17, I spoke on the phone with Bailie, the West Center administrator. She informed me that of the eighteen residents in Pecos House, eleven had tested positive for the coronavirus. Thankfully, Steve was not among them. He and the other men who had tested negative had been moved into the temporarily closed day program area to protect them from immediate possible spread. Of course, that did not mean they were completely safe. COVID was in the building and likely to stay. But for how long?

Before the scheduled update for all James L. West families via Zoom that evening, I took a short stroll through the neighborhood to clear my head. As I walked, the words from two old familiar hymns—"Trust and Obey" and "God of Grace and God of Glory"—kept finding their way in:

> *Trust and obey, for there's no other way*
> *To be happy in Jesus, but to trust and obey.*

> *Grant us wisdom, grant us courage,*
> *for the facing of this hour . . .*

I had no way of knowing then how many more times these lyrics would play over in my mind in the coming months.

At 5:00 p.m., I watched on my laptop as Bailie opened with a prayer and informed us that, in addition to the eleven men, one Pecos staff member had tested positive for COVID-19 as well.

Much to my surprise, Bailie personally called me shortly after the Zoom meeting ended. Things had changed rapidly. Steve now had a low-grade fever, which could be an indication of the virus. They were moving him back into his regular room alongside those residents who had tested positive. Over the next twenty-four hours, his oxygen level fell and his energy plummeted.

No longer was this the Alzheimer's roller-coaster ride I was used to. Now the cars were slamming into one another! I had emotional whiplash.

"Dear Lord," I prayed, "I know you will take Steve home to you when the time is right. Only, if at all possible, please, please don't let it be now."

Saying our final goodbye would be hard enough for the kids and me, I knew. But the thought of not being allowed to hold him close? Having no way for family and friends to come together to celebrate his life, share memories, and hear comforting words of scripture? Losing a precious loved one in that manner was too heartbreaking to imagine. Tragically, for hundreds of thousands of families, it became all too real. Blessedly, we were not one of them.

Four days later, on Tuesday, April 21, I was told, "Steve is back to being Steve."

Indeed, all the confirmed cases on his wing recovered. As Bailie said, "It was divine intervention."

Like rings on a child's stacking toy, halo upon halo was piled upon the care team members' heads over the next several months as the virus voraciously made its way through the units. Dutifully, they donned personal protective equipment (PPE) of medical gloves, gowns, and face masks. They scrubbed their hands until they were raw. On television, we heard reports about "tireless workers." There is no such thing. Thoroughly exhausted, the staff filled shifts for those who were unable to work due to symptoms of COVID-19, exposure to someone who had it, a positive test result, or utter burnout. Many isolated themselves from their families for fear of bringing the infection home. Additional staff members stayed after hours to Zoom call us with regular updates on everything from equipment shortages to resident morale— always ending in prayer. Despite all their sacrifices, they managed to smile with their eyes.

When Bailie asked family members to send notes of encouragement to the beleaguered staff, I willingly obliged by mailing a card or note every week for months. And whenever Kimberly posted an Amazon wish list for snacks to be delivered to the care team or requested monetary donations to provide staff lunches, I responded the best I could. The opportunity to be even the slightest bit helpful felt better than sitting by utterly helpless.

Along with the knowledge that Steve was receiving the best possible care, the only thing that made our physical distance bearable was receiving frequent video calls from the life enrichment team. Seeing Steve on my phone was extremely reassuring, and I began to feel close to the energetic women who made the calls. While residents at most other senior facilities were expected to wear masks and remain in their rooms, this was impossible with dementia care patients who were incapable of understanding the reasons why. Thus, framing Steve's unmasked face with a phone or tablet, kind staff members would match him, step for step, as he walked the hall in order to keep him in my view. They began looking forward to seeing Hays and Nora, who were sometimes in the picture with me.

"I love you, Stevie!" Hays would repeat after me.

When the call ended, he'd look at me and ask, "Is Stevie at work?" His grandfather clearly wasn't at home with me, and Hays was too young to remember visiting him in memory care.

"Yes, honey, he's at work," I said. It was a simple answer that made sense to his developing mind.

Throughout those months, those FaceTime calls were the highlight of many of my days. If I happened to be driving when a call came, I would pull over to the side of the road to answer. One morning, I talked to Steve while a green, moisturizing avocado mask dried on my cheeks. But imagine my surprise the afternoon I eagerly answered, only to discover another man's face staring at mine!

"Say hello to your wife," urged a woman's voice from off camera. I recognized it at once. It was a member of the life enrichment team, who had phoned me by mistake.

"That's not my wife," the resident growled.

As the staff member continued to encourage him, she must have been thinking how sad it was that this poor gentleman was so confused that he no longer could recognize his own wife.

"Yes, yes, say hello to your wife!" she repeated.

"That's *not* my wife!" he insisted.

After shaking my head and making silent gestures, finally I had to join in. "He's right. This is Kathe. I'm Steve's wife."

She quickly looked at the screen, said "Oh!" and hung up. I hoped the man was able to enjoy a video chat, minus the growls, with his own wife soon after.

Whenever my phone rang and the caller ID displayed James L. West *without* video, however, I held my breath for fear something had happened to Steve. Every now and then, it was a staff member calling to schedule our quarterly care conference or perhaps the doctor advising me of a change in his medications. More often, it was his nurse.

"Everything is okay," thankfully, is how she began each call.

Then I could exhale as she informed me that Steve had accidentally plopped to the floor when he barely missed the chair or that he had been in a "minor altercation" with another resident that resulted in a slight scratch or bruise. None of that was good, but at least, as she said, it was "okay." I had never expected perfection from a memory care facility, and I certainly wasn't going to start during a pandemic.

With restaurants closed except for takeout and delivery, my home became a hub for semi-regular family dinners and weekend brunches. Sometimes, I would cook. Other times, Stephen or Matt would grill. Occasionally, we would pick up curbside. Dinners were always preceded by a masterpiece of a cheese board, artfully arranged by Angela or Kelly. Every now and then, we were joined by my brother-in-law, Butch, and his soon-to-be fiancée, Elsie, who became part of our pod.

At the end of June, we welcomed happy, healthy baby Everett Goodwin. With the rising COVID-19 death toll at the top of every newscast, it was a truly wonderful gift to have a new life to celebrate. Although I wasn't allowed to be at the hospital—as I was when Angela delivered—I, along with the other happy grandparents and new aunts and uncles, was eagerly waiting at Kelly and Stephen's house when they brought their new baby home.

Even with all of that going on, I still—like many people—found myself with a lot of free time. Some of it was spent in deep thought, reflecting and reprioritizing. And some was essentially wasted.

When things first shut down, I pledged to every day reach out to someone, do something nice for someone, and exercise. After weeks of walking, sniffing, and peeing around our new neighborhood, Nora began hiding from the leash, much as she had at the old house following Angie's death. So much for that exercise plan! And it wasn't long before reaching out to someone by phone call or text became synonymous in my brain with doing something nice for them. Eventually, I exhausted my list of contacts. When one of those contacts unexpectedly called me on a Sunday evening, I realized she was the first human I had spoken to in twenty-four hours.

With Nora reluctant to be my exercise partner, I was thrilled to find an enthusiastic alternate in my Pilates instructor. She began teaching classes online, and I ordered a yoga mat so I could participate from home.

For the first time in my life, I binge-watched TV, starting with *The Crown* and moving through too many series to count. Some were better than others. Even so, who could stop midway? While I watched, I needlepointed and victoriously finished Hays's Christmas stocking several months early. Then I started one for Everett.

No longer able to sit around the mah-jongg table with friends, I addictively challenged the computerized version and very occasionally won.

Little things brought me more joy than I ever imagined. Cardinals, blue jays, woodpeckers, and other birds I still cannot identify alighted on the birdfeeder in my tiny garden morning and evening. They were beautiful and peaceful, and they sang to me. What an uplifting reminder of God's loving and caring nature. Several times, I took my laptop outside and watched them while participating in Kimberly's support groups, which were now held via Zoom.

And partly because of Kimberly, there was an idea I couldn't get out of my head. While she was the earthly nurturer of this book, and the pandemic gave it a growing season, I believe the Holy Spirit planted the seed . . .

Therefore encourage one another and build one another up,
just as you are doing.

(1 THESSALONIANS 5:11 RSV)

. . . and let us run with perseverance the race that is set
before us . . .

(HEBREWS 12:1 RSV)

Do not quench the Spirit . . .

(1 THESSALONIANS 5:19 NIV)

It seemed that each scripture was a call to action to share our family's story . . . even if it helped just one person. As 2 Corinthians 3:3 (RSV) says, I yearned to write "on tablets of human hearts." Yet little about the process came easily. I had to revisit all the raw places and open some old wounds. Many nights I lay sleepless as memories and words sprang into my head. I couldn't write them down fast enough. Other days, I simply couldn't face it. The Spirit was willing, but my flesh could be so weak. How could I depict our Alzheimer's journey through the lens of our Christian faith while honoring Steve's life? Was I really up to answering the call? Kimberly never failed to encourage. Angela and Stephen bolstered me with love and unending support. And the Lord listened to my continued prayers for his will and his words, often leading me to the perfect passage of scripture just when I needed it most.

As the summer of 2020 dwindled, visitation rules began changing at the West Center.

For months, many other facilities had allowed "window visits," where family members stood outside and communicated with their loved ones the best they could through the glass. Because of the structure of the West Center—with residents living solely on the second, third, and fourth floors—this was impossible. But the administrative staff at last devised a way.

Angela and I had our first window visit with Steve in mid-August. Only two family members were allowed at a time. Caregivers escorted him to the first-floor area off the employee parking lot where two floor-to-ceiling windows flanked a sliding glass door. It was the first time I had seen my husband head to toe in five months! He looked thin but still had most of his straight, brown hair and few facial wrinkles. His gait was more shuffle than step, and his posture was hunched in a way that reminded me of his late father. Communicating over cell phones and speakers, Angela and I told him through our tears how much we loved him and had missed him. Steve was happy and enthusiastic with his familiar disjointed words and sounds. Our allotted fifteen minutes ended much too swiftly. And when it was time to leave, Steve stood up and tried to open the glass door. He wanted to be with us as much as we wanted to be with him! As glorious as it was to see him, it was equally heartbreaking to have to stay at a distance, unable to embrace.

"Mom, can I bring Everett?" Stephen asked as his own window visit date soon approached.

"Let me think about that," I responded.

Only two visitors at a time was the rule. There were only two chairs under the small tent outside the window. But Stephen was a proud new father and anxious for Steve to finally meet his two-month-old grandson. And Everett certainly didn't need his own chair.

"Bring him. What are they going to say?"

It was the right thing to do, and a moment Stephen and I will cherish forever. No one said a word . . . other than how precious Everett was.

A few weeks later, just as visitation guidelines were beginning to evolve again, I awakened abruptly with a feeling I'd never had before.

CHAPTER 23

Timing . . .
Is Everything

There is a time for everything,
and a season for every activity under the heavens . . .

ECCLESIASTES 3:1 NIV

For all the emotional gut punches life had dealt me over the previous eight years, the internal gut punch I felt in the early morning hours of September 21, 2020, was a wrenching new experience. My abdomen was cramping in excruciating pain.

What was happening to me? This wasn't like the stomach flu I had before the Alzheimer's walk. There was something very different and very wrong. By 9:00 a.m., I texted Angela, who called immediately.

She had awakened in severe pain just two months earlier and had undergone an emergency appendectomy. "What did it feel like?" I asked her.

For a few minutes, we compared symptoms. While not exactly the same, there were enough similarities to sound the alarm. Angela promised to check back in on me and immediately notified her brother, who offered to take me to the hospital whenever I needed.

I called my doctor, who didn't call me back until after I left a second message. I called my health insurance carrier to ask which emergency room to go to. And then I waited . . . because I was expecting a furniture delivery between noon and four o'clock that afternoon. My beautiful new dining room buffet was already on the truck headed to my house, and I didn't know how to stop it. I threw on some clothes. I packed a small tote for the hospital. And then I waited some more . . . At three o'clock, the buffet finally arrived. I instantly hated the piece in person and wondered what possibly had compelled me to order it. Like so many of my online purchases in those days, it must have been the result of too much time on my hands and way too much of it spent at home. Immediately, I called Stephen and told him I was ready to go.

"What's your pain level, Mom?" he asked, watching me slowly, awkwardly climb into his SUV.

"An eight at least," I said.

"Wow, I never would have guessed that!" As I gripped the seat with one hand and my midsection with the other, I was thinking I should have said, "A nine!"

Although Stephen wanted to go into the hospital with me, I refused, encouraging him to go home to his family and promising to keep him and Angela updated. Based on past experience with hospitalized family members, I remembered the importance of bringing a phone charger. It was after 7:00 p.m. when the ER doctor determined that I indeed needed an appendectomy . . . but not until early the next morning! Until then, all I wanted was morphine. I learned that from Angela.

While in the ER, I was administered a preliminary COVID test. Then I had another, which the nurse said was the type required before surgery. Later as I slept in my hospital bed, I was awakened at 1:00 a.m. by a staff member who informed me that I had not yet taken the proper pre-surgery COVID test. That was the one that felt as if it went up to my brain. He hoped the results would come back before my procedure was scheduled. Me too.

What the surgeon found on the operating table that day wasn't pretty. My appendix was perforated. I was grateful it hadn't burst entirely.

Yet the whole experience gave me an opportunity to reflect on God's timing . . .

If Angela's appendicitis attack had hit a week before it did, she and Matt would have been paddling a canoe down the Brazos River with no cell phone service. If mine had come two weeks earlier, she, Hays, and I would have been speeding down a lonely highway on our return from a long weekend in a cabin in tiny Broken Bow, Oklahoma. I thanked the Lord that neither of those scenarios came to pass.

And I realized why the Lord had compelled me to change out the flowers at the cemetery the day before I awakened in such pain. The pull to the gravesite that Sunday was so undeniable that I half expected to hear Angie's voice, as I had before, or to experience some other heavenly encounter. But I left there with a shrug of my shoulders and a shake of my head, a little disappointed that there had been no lightning bolt. Now sitting in my hospital bed, I realized the bolt had come in the form of appendicitis. And I was relieved and happy that I had already placed the autumn purple flowers, an homage to Angie's beloved TCU Horned Frogs, where they needed to dwell for the remainder of football season.

Adhering to COVID restrictions, the hospital allowed me only one visitor per day. The kids took turns staying with me for a few hours each of the four days I was recovering there, even though I insisted that I was quite accustomed to being by myself since I'd lived alone for years. It's true that if we live long enough, the parent-child roles reverse. Still, I wasn't quite ready for the feeling I had when Angela held *my* hair back while I vomited into a bag.

If a video call came from the West Center while I was in the hospital, I don't remember it. I hope there weren't any. Even without the aid of an avocado mask, my face was decidedly green. I didn't want Steve to be frightened by what he saw.

On the day of my dismissal, I requested Angela send a pair of my loosest pants and a roomy T-shirt with Stephen, who had mom-sitting duty that afternoon. Just lying in bed and taking short walks down the hall in my hospital gown, I was keenly aware my abdomen was extremely swollen from surgery. But struggling with my "fat pants" in the bathroom, I realized my thighs were enormous too.

"We can't get pants on Steve!" I remembered the nurse telling me months before. Now the question was, "How do I get pants on Kathe?" It wasn't easy.

While I was in the hospital, Stephen went to my house to feed Nora and let her out a couple of times a day. When that big labradoodle ran out of food—as she often does—Beckie, my cherished friend and close neighbor, went out and bought more. She even rummaged in my cabinets to find Nora's harness and leash to take her on a few walks around the block. I remain most grateful.

Once I was home, precious family and more loyal friends sprang into action. Realizing that one old, green fleece robe was the only thing in my closet that fit comfortably, I asked Patti to buy me a couple of very large nightgowns, which she readily did. Mary Claire brought over homemade custard, still warm from her oven, to help the antibiotics go down. And in true Texas fashion, others sent various forms of comfort food . . .

"I'm bringing you a milkshake!"

"How about a twice-baked potato or some mac and cheese?"

"I left a basket of baked goodies at your front door."

"When may I bring you lunch?"

How blessed I felt to have such a wonderful support system!

During my recuperation, restrictions at the West Center began to change. The doors were *finally* going to reopen to family members! However, the only way in was to jump over numerous new hurdles.

Just two people per resident would be considered "essential caregivers" with visiting privileges. Unquestionably, in our family, one of them would be me. But we had two children. It was a bit of a *Sophie's Choice*, yet thankfully without the dire consequences. I let the kids decide. Because Stephen had a more flexible work schedule, they concluded that he should be their father's other essential caregiver.

In order to visit Steve, we were required to:

- Watch training videos on proper handwashing and the wearing of PPE
- Wear an N95 or KN95 mask
- Make appointments within predetermined blocks of time
- Restrict our visits to a maximum of two per week
- Have our temperature checked upon arrival
- Provide proof of a negative COVID test within the past fourteen days (which soon changed to seven)
- Be escorted to the proper house by a designated staff member

Although not specified, we were also required to wear actual clothes. While I would have crawled over hot coals to see Steve after all those lost months, no one wanted to see me do that in a nightgown. And so I waited until I could fit into something appropriate for public wear.

At last, that day arrived. As I was escorted to the door of Pecos House, I was unsure what to expect on the other side. Thanks to coveted video calls and window visits, I assumed Steve would still know me. But since this would be his first time seeing me in a face mask, I wondered whether that would change. How different would the atmosphere feel after everything the care team had been through? Would my favorites still be there? How had the other residents fared, having been isolated for so long? My heart was jittery with anticipation . . .

Then there was my beloved Steve! Just beyond the nurses' station! When I stepped into his sightline, his eyes glistened with tears and his smile showed a newly chipped front tooth. Without hesitation, he wrapped his arms around me. Not quite a bear hug anymore, it was great in its gentleness.

"I la-la-love you!" he said.

"I love you, too," I answered as I looked up into those green eyes.

I was still his Baby Girl, and it felt life-affirming to tenderly touch his cheek once again.

Lord, please give me time to soak in this moment, I silently prayed.

That was not to be. Quickly, we were guided into his room, where we were asked to remain for the duration of our visit. Throughout all his years in memory care, Steve had never been content to stay in his room. Why should that change today? I understood the thinking that our seclusion would minimize any risk of my exposing other residents to the virus. But Steve didn't understand that. So out his door we went.

I tried to find a couple of chairs in a common area where no one else was lingering. That worked for a few minutes until he stood up and began roaming the hall. They didn't want me doing that, so I had to leave. This uncomfortable scene repeated itself many times over. But at least I got to hold his hand, if only for a few moments.

And what a trembling hand it was. There were several changes in him since my last visit in March, and this was one of them. Whether Steve was lying in his bed, sitting in the living area, walking the hallway, or eating a meal, his hands and legs often quivered. During the pandemic, windows frequently were kept open for ventilation. I thought he might be cold. But when we moved away from the window, the shaking continued. In a care conference, I asked if it could be a side effect of medication. I was told that was possible, and then the subject was dismissed until I inquired again.

"Have you seen him drink a glass of cranberry juice without spilling a drop?" a nurse asked me. Yes, I had, but I always felt we were just one quiver away from a big, wet, red mess.

Clearly, no one shared my level of concern. I was puzzled. Sometimes I could still the movement with a soft, steady touch. And sometimes the quivering started the moment I nestled beside him. With no ready explanation, I told myself he was alternately soothed and excited by my presence.

Eventually, I asked Steve's doctor if he could have Parkinson's disease. She said no, explaining that his tremor, shuffling gait, and rigidity were most likely caused by Parkinsonism. In the same way that dementia is a broad term encompassing many diseases including Alzheimer's, Parkinsonism is a general term referring to a group of neurological disorders that cause movement problems similar to those seen in patients with Parkinson's disease. The doctor told me that Parkinsonism occurs in more than half of patients in the later stages of Alzheimer's as neurodegeneration takes effect in the brain. Unfortunately, Alzheimer's patients do not respond favorably to Parkinson's medications. Another fact willingly learned. Another change begrudgingly accepted.

A further development I noticed was Steve's incessant humming. Nothing resembling a recognizable tune, it was more like the hum of an electric dishwasher with a human voice, adding short pauses for breaths. And like the trembling hand, sometimes my presence turned it on; other times, it turned it off. At this stage of his disease, no one could tell me if that was coincidental or not, whether the humming was a calming or coping mechanism, or if it was merely compulsive behavior. A few of the other residents heard it too and mimicked the sound when they were close by. I'm unsure if they were mocking him or if his humming simply put the idea into their heads.

Also, Steve had lost weight. His clothes were now ill-fitting, and so I shopped for more—unfolding them, eyeballing their lengths, and fully extending their waistbands in the hopes of selecting the proper size. No longer did I purchase khaki pants; we'd now fully transitioned to those with elastic, drawstring waists.

Shoes were another concern. Pairs were separated, and other men's slippers frequently found their way onto Steve's feet. The ones he owned were too large, and I incorrectly assumed they were just stretched out too much. After many failed purchases, I realized his foot had shrunk. Not surprisingly, when we played Cinderella and I placed the right-sized shoes on his feet, he shuffled a little less. And just as Cinderella smartly kept the mate to her lost glass slipper, I came up with an idea of my own. Why not buy two or three pairs of slippers for Steve, all in the same style and color? That way, if a mate went missing here or there, it would still be relatively easy to have a matching pair. I wondered why I hadn't thought of that sooner.

Ultimately, the staff gave up on their impossible efforts to confine Steve and me to his room. Together, we were allowed to sit in a corner of the living area, far removed from the other residents. We were allowed to walk the Pecos hallway so long as we socially distanced from everyone else. And we were allowed to sit by ourselves at a remote table at lunch. Considering the required masks, temperature checks, escorts, appointments, and now *weekly* COVID-19 tests, this was as normal as it was going to get for a while.

Getting a COVID test at a nearby site, receiving the results, and scheduling a visit within a seven-day period became a three-piece juggling act. I learned how to spit in a tube in my car, swab my cheeks in a parking lot tent, and eventually shove a stick up each nostril in the James L. West lobby. If I took my COVID test on a Tuesday and only possibly received the results by Thursday evening, my appointment better be scheduled for Friday, Saturday, or Sunday. No visitors allowed on Monday or Tuesday. And no more than two visitors could be in any wing at any time. So even when I managed to keep all the pieces aloft to schedule a visitation, I sometimes did not receive my top-choice time slot if others claimed it first. All of this made it nearly impossible for Stephen to visit, as he had a juggling act of his own with work, a wife, and a baby. Still, we managed to do it together—juggling twice the number of balls—a couple of times.

Unfortunately, one of those visits became a lesson in what *not* to do. After all these months, I couldn't begin to imagine how many days Steve had gone without being outdoors in fresh air. On this beautiful afternoon—when we confirmed that no one else had reserved the courtyard—Stephen and I decided to take his dad outside to the gazebo. Volunteering to be our escort, one of our favorite caregivers helped coax Steve into the elevator for the ride to the ground floor. We guided him slowly to the sliding glass doors. They opened automatically just where the carpet under our feet turned to tile, and he would not willingly cross that threshold. I don't know if it was the doors, the flooring, fear of the unknown, or something else, but we certainly weren't going to force him to do something he clearly didn't want to do.

Thus we pivoted to Plan B. Back on the elevator, we were escorted up to the second-floor terrace. Once there, it took only a few minutes for Stephen and me to realize that the bright sun was hurting Steve's eyes. So we moved into the shade, where he rapidly became chilled. By the time we all returned to Pecos, our appointment window was over. We had wasted our precious hour moving about and doing what we thought would be good for Steve rather than simply allowing ourselves to just *be*.

For me and millions of others, the holiday season of 2020 was like none we'd ever experienced before or hoped to experience again.

Because health officials warned us against gathering in large groups, our pod made the difficult decision not to join extended family for Thanksgiving dinner at Patti and Jody's. It was the only occasion of the year when we had all planned to be together, so as Stephen carved our little turkey in my kitchen, we couldn't help feeling disappointed.

During the week of Christmas, I happily visited Steve on the twenty-fourth. But Christmas Day itself consisted of ever-changing last-minute plans. One by one, members of our semi-extended pod informed me they weren't coming to my house after all out of fear of COVID exposure and "an abundance of caution." Thus, I placed plastic to-go containers of too much food alongside an array of wrapped gifts on my front porch for assigned family members to pick up.

How could I possibly feel sorry for myself on my Savior's birthday? But I did. In tears, I called Angela, who quickly notified Stephen. Although both were spending the day with their in-laws—as we alternated holidays each year—they came running to my rescue.

"Mom, you will *never* be alone on Christmas Day!" Stephen reassured me.

"You'll always have us," Angela said, as she poured the wine that I had uncorked for the no-shows.

With that, I realized how blessed Steve and I were to have these sensitive adult children, how much I missed their father, and how unexpectedly special this evening had turned out to be.

I also realized that instead of feeling sorry for myself, I should have been reflecting on how fortunate our family had been over the past ten months. In the midst of quarantines, hospitalizations, and deaths from COVID-19, none of us, including Steve, had caught the virus. While hundreds of thousands had died as a direct result of the virus itself, countless others—especially those in long-term care facilities—had experienced COVID-related deaths from feelings of depression, abandonment, and hopelessness. No one, from the top decision-makers down, had known how best to handle this pandemic. It was, as government officials, medical experts, and journalists continually reminded us, "unprecedented."

As New Year's Eve approached, the media was filled with references to the saying "hindsight is 20/20"—or in this case, "2020." That was how we all wanted to see the past year . . . in hindsight.

CHAPTER 24

What Now, My Lord?

For this slight momentary affliction is preparing us
for an eternal weight of glory beyond all comparison,
because we look not to the things that are seen
but to the things that are unseen;
for the things that are seen are transient,
but the things that are unseen are eternal.

2 CORINTHIANS 4:17–18 RSV

Much like the effect of Alzheimer's on the brain, the year 2020 seemed like a tablet that, once dropped in water, slowly began to fizzle out until there was nothing left. No longer was it a matter of seeing the glass as half-empty or half-full—we needed a new glass. Welcome, 2021.

For millions, this new glass was filled with hope in the form of a COVID-19 vaccine. When it became available to Steve, along with the other West Center residents and staff, I signed the consent form without hesitation. The thought of going through another year like the previous one was beyond comprehension. Thus, when my own turn came in February, I couldn't get to the vaccination site fast enough ... twice. Each member of our family pod eagerly followed suit.

Month by month, our lives began to feel a little bit safer, more secure, more—dare I say—"normal." I was thrilled to be with Steve on his birthday once again. After a year of working at home, Stephen was able to reconnect with coworkers face-to-face in his company's shining new office space, which had closed its doors almost before they opened in March 2020. Houses of worship again welcomed in-person congregations. Once more, weddings were cheerfully celebrated with extended families and friends, and the lives of deceased loved ones were commemorated as they should be. As we were able to come together, we waved goodbye for now to drive-by birthday parties and virtual baby showers. Unmasked at last, my mah-jongg group gathered once more around my table to play. It felt good to hug one another again.

During this time, our county COVID-19 positivity rate continued to change, and medical and governmental guidelines for long-term residential facilities were often modified. Dutifully, the West Center team always notified us promptly via Zoom. Do-it-yourself, rapid nose swab COVID tests eventually became available at the center, which greatly simplified the juggling act that was previously required to visit. One day, even those instant tests became unnecessary. Soon, an escort to the wing was no longer mandated. And finally, I could see my Steve without an appointment. So could Stephen and Angela. Each unstructured visit was a Hallelujah Day!

But one evening, a few weeks before those last regulations were lifted, I received an unsettling phone call.

"May I speak with Mrs. Goodwin?" asked the nurse on Pecos.

"Yes, this is she," I responded.

"Everything is okay," she assured me as usual. Except this time, it really wasn't.

"Steve was resting, and another resident pulled him out of bed," she told me, adhering to the rule of withholding the other man's name. "He hit his head on the nightstand, and he screamed. We rushed in immediately, and we will do an evaluation."

Tears of compassion cascaded down my cheeks. Of course he screamed! I would too! What a terrifying way to be awakened from a peaceful sleep. I knew the nurse meant they would do a medical evaluation . . . but how about an evaluation of how this was allowed to happen? My emotions quickly got the better of me, yet I could not bring myself to unburden myself on anyone—not Patti, not Mary Claire or Beckie, and certainly not the children. If I could have, I would have called my sister. That thought made me all the more emotional.

I prayed for Steve. Then as I regained control over my feelings, I began to reflect. First, I thought about my sweet visit with him earlier that day. He had devoured three cookies and an ice cream sandwich, which I was glad to see. We had hugged and held hands as we walked the hall before I left him napping in his bed. Next, however, I remembered all the times I had found Steve in someone else's bed. And I recounted the numerous occasions he'd become combative when another resident had dared to enter his room. This was just another step along that same pathway. Only this time, the footprints weren't Steve's. I prayed for the other resident—whoever it was. And I forgave him as others had forgiven Steve. Love the man; hate the disease.

Since restrictions had loosened following COVID's known zenith, the West Center had welcomed several new residents to Pecos and to the other houses. I soon realized that Steve's new neighbors were experiencing many of the same behaviors that had brought him there more than two years prior. Such was the case with the man who had yanked him out of bed. And such was the case with the man who approached Steve and me as we sat quietly side by side on the living area sofa one day.

Waving his hands about and spewing word salad, the man grinned mischievously and laughed as he came within an inch of slapping Steve across the face.

"He's just kidding, honey," I said, placing my hand firmly on my husband's thigh in an attempt to prevent any backlash.

But I immediately discovered that I didn't need to do a thing. Whereas the *old* Steve would have sprung to his feet in anger or at least grabbed the man's hand, this *new* Steve, in a progressed stage of Alzheimer's, did not even flinch.

Unsure what to make of all this, I was glad my quarterly care conference was scheduled for the next day. On the Zoom call, Linda, the West Center assistant director of nursing, expressed her shared concerns, acknowledging that Steve now seemed placid and complacent. While that might have been a welcome relief in the past, it wasn't working to his benefit in the current Pecos environment.

"I am a little worried for his safety," she confided. "He appears unable or uninterested in defending himself."

When I asked about possibly moving him to another wing, she readily agreed it was a good idea. Once again, however, I should have guessed that God had a better plan in the works . . .

A lateral move. That was what I wanted for Steve. Just across the third-floor hall to Red River House, where male and female residents were in mid-stage dementia. Because visitors were still not allowed to move freely about the West Center, Linda escorted me there and gave me a quick tour. I met a few members of the staff, said hello to some of the residents, and was pleased with what I observed. Then Linda hit me with a bombshell.

"Perhaps we should go upstairs and see Trinity," she suggested.

That was the fourth floor, the wing for patients in the final stages, the place where my father had died. It hadn't occurred to me that Steve was ready for *that*. It hadn't occurred to me that *I* might need to be.

"Okay, if you think so," I responded. Following her through that door was every bit as hard as I thought it would be.

When my tour ended, Linda encouraged me to take my time in considering both options. The consensus was that Steve, with his now calm demeanor, no longer needed a private room. But because of his wandering, a room with a bed closest to the door was preferable. Both houses had such rooms available. The decision was entirely up to me.

Once again, I called on the Lord before calling Kimberly. I was relieved to see how up to date she was on Steve's condition amid the changing Pecos atmosphere. She said she had noticed his face often had a "flat affect," by which she meant a severe reduction in emotional expressions.

"When are you next scheduled to visit Steve?" she asked.

"Tomorrow at two," I told her.

"If you can meet me at one, I will take you back to both houses," she willingly offered.

"Thank you so much. I'll be there!"

First we went to Red River. It was livelier than it had been when I visited the day before. A large group of residents was gathered around an energetic team member whose voice carried down the hall. In celebration of Stevie Wonder's birthday, his face and his music were on the TV. As she handed out fact sheets on the entertainer, the caregiver highlighted facets of his life. Her audience seemed enthralled. Some even followed along on the fact sheet. No one got restless and left. As much as my own wonderful Steve loved the music of Stevie Wonder, it all felt a little too complex for him at this stage of the disease. And Kimberly hinted that, if I chose to place him there, it might only be a matter of a few months before a move upstairs became imperative.

When we entered Trinity, the environment was calming. Ever since Steve first moved into the West Center, the fact that all the wings had been remodeled and renamed since my parents lived there had kept me from constantly reliving those difficult days. This was even truer of Trinity. It was lighter, more open, and felt more welcoming than it had six years prior.

A waterfall wall greeted us while familiar Motown tunes played softly in the background. I saw fish swimming in large and small tanks, and I met Butterball the bunny. On this floor, there was easy access to a small outdoor terrace.

As I watched caregivers individually interact with residents, Kimberly explained that the ratio of staff to patient was higher here than in Red River. That was important to me since Steve and many others often needed mealtime assistance. She introduced me to the nurse on duty and a life enrichment team member, who showed me the Namaste room with its comfortable lounge chairs, soft lighting, and soothing aromatherapy.

But when Kimberly pointed out the one room with an available bed closest to the door, I could not believe my eyes.

"It's a sign," I acknowledged.

The room number was 407, the street address of my childhood home and the house my parents lived in for sixty-four years.

As I rode the elevator back to the third floor, I marveled how things were falling into place in a way that I hadn't imagined. The words of Isaiah 55:8–9 (NIV) came into my head:

> *"For my thoughts are not your thoughts, neither are your ways my ways,"*
> *declares the Lord. "As the heavens are higher than the earth, so are my*
> *ways higher than your ways and my thoughts than your thoughts."*

When I opened the door to Pecos, the nurse intercepted me before I could reach the closed door to Steve's private room.

"I just want to warn you that there is another man in there with Steve," she said. "They are in the bed together, and both are sleeping soundly above the covers."

Just when I thought I had seen and heard it all . . . But I hadn't seen anything yet. After knocking lightly, the nurse opened Steve's door, revealing undeniably that he and another resident were sleeping in his bed. However, that wasn't the only thing that was revealed. Somehow the other man had managed to undress himself and was now completely naked! No one was more shocked than the nurse, who quickly called for assistance and shut the door until they could put clothes on the man and awaken Steve. With sincere apologies to me, they finally brought Steve out of the room. He seemed completely unfazed.

While the two of us sat holding hands on the sofa, a tall, thin woman quietly approached me. Because she and I, like all visitors and staff, were wearing face masks, I could see only her kind eyes,

"Are you Kathe?" she inquired. "We talked on the phone a while back."

"Oh, yes!" I responded, glad to finally connect in person.

Several months earlier, I'd been asked by the director of admissions to visit with prospective families about our experience at the West Center. When this woman had called me, she was still caring for her husband at home and considering moving him into memory care. Now he was living in the room next door to Steve.

"My husband is the one who pulled Steve out of his bed," she voluntarily told me.

That moment was yet another climax in a day already full of them.

"It's so nice to meet you. I wish we'd met here earlier," I told her. "I think we are moving Steve upstairs soon."

CHAPTER 25

Trinity

And the Lord said to him,
"Take off the shoes from your feet,
for the place where you are standing is holy ground."

ACTS 7:33 RSV

From the moment Steve moved to Trinity, I realized we were on holy ground. It was a realization I should have come to long before ... If it were not for holy ground beneath our feet on our entire Alzheimer's journey, we would forever have been stuck in a quagmire of fear and doubt. Now, once again, we were moving forward.

Like the other houses in the West Center, Trinity paid tribute to a Texas river. The fact that the Trinity River runs through Fort Worth made this wing's name all the more special.

But I sensed it was more than that. Here I felt the gift, the blessing, the very essence of God in three persons—the Father, the Son, and the Spirit—the Holy Trinity. We were in church. Even the decorative panels in the hallway resembled stained glass windows. And just as church may ring with the sounds of laughter, uplifting music, and clapping hands, or alternatively serve as a sanctuary for solemnity, tears, and hands folded in prayer, so it was with Trinity. Life was revered; death was mourned. I know why this house is on the top floor of the building. It's the closest to heaven.

When Angela and Stephen visited, followed shortly by Mary Claire and Beckie, they too were comforted by what they saw and how they felt in Steve's new environment. Soon after Beckie's visit, she wrote me this note:

> *Thank you for allowing me the privilege of going with you to see Steve last week. He is such a wonderful man, and it was a joy to see him again. I will always cherish witnessing the love in his eyes when he looks at you. Touched my heart deeply.*

Her words touched my heart as well, especially as I remembered our family's darkest days when there was anything but love for me in my husband's eyes. As sorry as I was to witness the debilitating progression of Steve's disease, I was glad those days were behind us.

Only a week into his adjustment to Trinity, Steve began sleeping . . . a lot. Not only did he sleep through the night, but he also napped for long periods before and after meals, and even nodded off during them. I was concerned.

Was it that he felt safer and more relaxed in this new environment? Surely, it was quieter than Pecos with almost no altercations and few verbal outbursts. With the vast majority of the residents here in wheelchairs, he didn't need to worry as much about one of them forcibly pulling him out of his bed or snuggling up to him uninvited. The bigger threat was that one might inadvertently run over his toes.

Alternatively, could this possibly be a turning point in the disease? Persons in advanced stages of dementia tend to sleep much of the time. They stop eating. And because of Steve's grogginess, he was incredibly unsteady on his feet. More than once, a caregiver or I had to scoot a chair up behind him to keep him from falling. I asked about having him fitted for a wheelchair.

Might his constant sleepiness be a side effect of some medication? Back when Steve was more easily agitated and combative, drugs had been needed to calm him and keep him at baseline as much as possible. Now that he had moved through that phase of the disease, could the drugs be bringing him down too far below baseline?

Most likely, it was a combination of all three. But when they began cutting back on his medication, Steve started coming back to us. He ate. He counted to ten with the speech therapist. And although his posture was incredibly stooped, he was more sure-footed. He began roaming the house as he had in Pecos.

"Steve's wandering into other residents' rooms doesn't really seem to bother anyone in Trinity," Linda assured me on a care conference call.

"If anything, the ladies sort of like it!" she laughed.

One of these ladies rolled up beside us in the hallway where we were hugging one afternoon. As Steve loudly said to me, "I love you!" she sweetly touched my arm.

Looking up into my eyes from her wheelchair, she repeated four words over and over. I was unsure whether she was saying, "You are his fate," or "You are his faith." Either way, her beautiful sentiment affirmed Beckie's heartfelt observation. And I marveled at how this elderly resident, in an advanced stage of dementia, could possibly understand Steve's abiding trust in me and find the words to express her feelings. Once again, I was made aware of how little we truly know about what is happening inside the brain.

On one morning visit, I arrived just as the music therapist was leaving Trinity. With a smile, she told me Steve had been dancing with a member of the life enrichment team, twirling her around and around until she could spin no more.

"That's my guy!" I happily confirmed.

Without a doubt, however, the best day came when I was allowed to finally take off my mask. Because we were both vaccinated against COVID-19—but some of the other residents and staff members were not—I was permitted to unmask only when we were alone in his room together. I couldn't begin to imagine how he would feel seeing my whole face in person after sixteen seemingly endless months! When I gently pressed my lips to his cheek as he slept in his bed, he opened his eyes, blinked, and smiled. In a fractured fairy-tale sort of way, I had at long last awakened my sleeping prince with a kiss.

Looking back, rewriting the fairy tale was nothing new to our family. In our story, my Prince Charming frequently fell short of his name. And, regretfully, I often resembled a wicked queen more than a demure princess. As previous chapters have revealed, each of our characters wrestled with the unfolding plot in our own time, in our own way. There were moments when I couldn't envision how we might possibly emerge from what seemed like the deepest and darkest of dungeons. But then the tiniest flicker would illuminate a path we hadn't seen before. We shifted our focus to what Steve *could* do rather than what he couldn't. We offered one another shoulders to lean on and hands to lift each other up out of the shadowy places. We tried to remember to laugh. And we continually prayed for guidance, for comfort, and for strength.

Sadly, the villain in our fairy tale is far more frightening than those in storybooks and movies. It has no horns, fangs, or claws, but the ugliest of faces. It does not possess a magical mirror, foreboding spell, or enchanted sword, but threatens with something much more sinister—plaques and tangles in the brain. This villain steals. It destroys. And it kills. Its name is Alzheimer's. There is no fortress that can protect against it, no weapons that can defeat it.

Yet in the wake of its destruction—in true fairy-tale fashion—our villain unintentionally left us with surprising gifts. Without Alzheimer's disease, I doubt that I would be known affectionately as Steve's "Baby Girl." I would never have heard him repeatedly and proudly proclaim, "Kathe is my life!" Today, listening to him utter his own garbled version of "I love you" is sweeter to my ears than the first time he clearly whispered it to me when I was a twenty-two-year-old girl with a crush.

Will I be despondent when he stops saying those words? Definitely. Will I be heartsick when he no longer recognizes me? More than I can say. Will I grieve when his body breathes its last? With Angela and Stephen held close in my arms.

Still, no matter what the future holds, our faith that dug deeper, our hope that reached higher, our love that grew stronger, and our everlasting joy will remain. The villainous Alzheimer's thief cannot steal these from us. And, praise God, together one day Steve and I will have our fairy-tale ending . . . living *happily ever after* in his heavenly kingdom.

Until that day, we are blessed to be dwelling on holy ground.

And I am profoundly grateful that love, in its own way, remembers.

They have no speech, they use no words;
no sound is heard from them.
Yet their voice goes out into all the earth,
their words to the ends of the world.

PSALM 19:3–4 NIV

May 2015 Photo credit: Richard Hill

Acknowledgments

With a grateful and humble heart, I thank God for his many gifts, especially the extraordinary people he has placed in my life.

Angela and Stephen, you are your father's shining stars and the light of my world. Your openness, honesty, and courage, as reflected in these pages, far exceeds anything I could have imagined. While losing your dad, you've found amazing inner strength. I am so proud of you both! Thank you for being you, for bringing Matt and Kelly into our lives, and for my precious grandchildren whom I adore.

Additional loving family and loyal friends, you have blessed me beyond words. Without listing each of your names, I trust you know who you are and hope you know how much I cherish you. Long before our Alzheimer's journey began, you were standing by our side. Today, you stand with us still. Thank you for your continued phone calls, texts, emails, invitations, notes, visits, and prayers. And thank you for being unafraid to ask, "How is Steve? How are the kids? How are you?" even though sometimes I am unsure how to respond. For those of you now struggling with a dementia diagnosis in your own family, I pray I can be as good a friend to you as you have been to me.

Memory care team partners through the years, you have touched Steve's life and mine in remarkably positive ways. Our quality of life is better because of you. Thank you for showing us what living up to a higher calling truly looks like.

Every participant in every caregiver support group that I have been privileged to attend, you are my heroes. I've learned from you. I've laughed with you. I've cried with you. Most of all, I have admired you. Ours is a path no one would willingly choose, but the steps are a bit easier when we take them together.

Finally, Kimberly, you never stopped believing this was a book that should be written. Without your unfailing encouragement and support, it would forever be just an idea circling over a runway. Thank you for being my copilot and bringing it in for a safe landing.

About the Author

Kathe Ambrose Goodwin is a graduate of Texas Christian University, where she majored in journalism and English, and of Southern Methodist University, where she earned a master's degree in mass communications. For many years, she worked in advertising and public relations. Today, Kathe is a proud wife, mother, and grandmother. A lifelong resident of Fort Worth, Texas, she is a member of First United Methodist Church, Junior League, The Assembly, Lecture Foundation, Kappa Kappa Gamma, and Phi Beta Kappa, as well as a former board member of the Gladney Center for Adoption. Kathe has been a featured panelist at dementia seminars sponsored by the TCU Harris College of Nursing, James L. West Center for Dementia Care, and Dementia Friendly Fort Worth, and she serves on the HSC Center for Older Adults Nursing Home Advisory Council.

Suggested Resources
For Education and Support

Alzheimer's Association (www.alz.org)

James L. West Center for Dementia Care (www.jameslwest.org)

Rosalynn Carter Institute for Caregivers (www.rosalynncarter.org)

Dementia Friendly Fort Worth (dffw.org)

Positive Approach to Care (teepasnow.com)

Dementia Action Alliance (www.daanow.org)